EASTER

Proclamation

Interpreting the Lessons of the Church Year

L. William Countryman

EASTER

PROCLAMATION 6 | SERIES C

FORTRESS PRESS | MINNEAPOLIS

BS
391.2
.P756
Series
c/5

PROCLAMATION 6
Interpreting the Lessons of the Church Year
Series C, Easter

Copyright © 1997 Augsburg Fortress. All rights reserved. Except for brief quotations in critical articles or reviews, no part of this book may be reproduced in any manner without prior written permission of the publisher. Write to: Augsburg Fortress, Box 1209, Minneapolis, MN 55440.

Scripture quotations, unless otherwise indicated, are from the New Revised Standard Version Bible, copyright © 1989 by the Division of Christian Education of the National Council of Churches in the U.S.A. and are used by permission.

Cover design: Ellen Maly
Text design: David Lott

The Library of Congress has cataloged the first four volumes of Series A as follows:

Proclamation 6, Series A: interpreting the lessons of the church
year.
    p.   cm.
    Contents: [1] Advent/Christmas / J. Christiaan Beker — [2] Epiphany / Susan K. Hedahl — [3] Lent / Peter J. Gomes — [4] Holy Week / Robin Scroggs.
    ISBN 0-8006-4207-4 (v. 1 : alk. paper) — ISBN 0-8006-4208-2 (v. 2 : alk. paper) — ISBN 0-8006-4209-0 (v. 3 : alk. paper) — ISBN 0-8006-4210-4 (v. 4 : alk. paper).
    1. Bible—Homiletical use. 2. Bible—liturgical lessons, English.
BS534.5P74   1995
251—dc20   95-4622
                                                                                          CIP
    Series C:
    Advent/Christmas / E. Elizabeth Johnson—ISBN 0-8006-4231-7
    Epiphany / Richard I. Pervo—ISBN 0-8006-4232-5
    Lent / Bernhard W. Anderson —ISBN 0-8006-4233-3
    Holy Week / Patricia Wilson-Kastner—ISBN 0-8006-4234-1
    Easter / L. William Countryman—ISBN 0-8006-4235-X
    Pentecost 1 / Terence E. Fretheim—ISBN 0-8006-4236-8
    Pentecost 2 / James L. Boyce—ISBN 0-8006-4237-6
    Pentecost 3 / William L. Holladay—ISBN 0-8006-4238-4

The paper used in this publication meets the minimum requirements of American National Standard for Information Sciences—Permanence of Paper for Printed Library Materials, ANSI Z329.48-1948.

Manufactured in the U. S. A.   AF 1-4235

    01   00   99   98   97   1   2   3   4   5   6   7   8   9   10

Contents

Introduction	7
Easter Day *The Resurrection of Our Lord*	8
Easter Evening or Easter Monday *The Resurrection of Our Lord*	15
Second Sunday of Easter	20
Third Sunday of Easter	26
Fourth Sunday of Easter	32
Fifth Sunday of Easter	37
Sixth Sunday of Easter	42
The Ascension of Our Lord	48
Seventh Sunday of Easter	54
Pentecost Sunday *The Day of Pentecost/Whitsunday*	59

Introduction

The broad pattern of the Eastertide lections is that the Gospel readings are drawn from John, the second lessons from Revelation, and the first lessons from Acts. The readings are on parallel tracks, not closely coordinated with each other. Some Sundays, however, do have "themes." The Second Sunday of Easter is traditionally associated with the story of Thomas's doubts, the Fourth with the Good Shepherd discourses, while the last two Sundays of Easter look forward to the Ascension and Pentecost. In the present volume, I have followed a general pattern of treating the lessons in reverse order (Gospel, second lesson, first lesson), except for Ascension Day and Pentecost, when the centrality of the lessons from Acts called for different procedures.

I have given preference in my commentary to literary and spiritual aspects of interpretation. I have called attention to literary elements, both within the lessons and in their context, that help to disclose the structure of each passage and what points it emphasizes. I have also called attention to what the lesson expects by way of response from the faithful hearer. How does it expect the hearer to grow, move, turn? What form does the gospel's call for conversion (*metanoia*) take?

Throughout the Easter season, the proclamation of Jesus' resurrection is central. This event is shown as bewildering, disorienting, and life changing. I have emphasized this and the attendant themes of joy and hope, which the resurrection of Jesus makes possible for the believer even in apparently desperate circumstances.

For my understanding of the lections from the Gospel of John, I have drawn heavily on my own previous studies, embodied in *The Mystical Way in the Fourth Gospel* (rev. ed.; Valley Forge, Pa.: Trinity Press International, 1994). The New Testament quotations in this volume are my own translations. The Old Testament quotations are taken from the New Revised Standard Version.

Easter Day
The Resurrection of Our Lord

Lectionary	First Lesson	Psalm	Second Lesson	Gospel
Revised Common	Acts 10:34-43 or Isa. 65:17-25	Ps. 118:1-2, 14-24	1 Cor. 15:19-26 or Acts 10:34-43	John 20:1-18 or Luke 24:1-12
Episcopal (BCP)	Acts 10:34-43 or Isa. 51:9-11	Ps. 118:14-29 or 118:14-17, 22-24	Col. 3:1-4 or Acts 10:34-43	Luke 24:1-10
Roman Catholic	Acts 10:34a, 37-43	Ps. 118:1-2, 16-17, 22-24	Col. 3:1-4 or 1 Cor. 5:6-8	John 20:1-9
Lutheran (LBW)	Exod. 15:1-11 or Ps. 118:14-24	Ps. 118:1-2, 15-24	1 Cor. 15:1-11	Luke 24:1-11 or John 20:1-9, (10-18)

The Resurrection of Jesus is utterly familiar, since it is the key affirmation of Christian faith, but it never loses its startling quality. In New Testament accounts of meetings with the risen Lord, two basic affirmations keep reappearing: first, it was really Jesus that people met after the resurrection; second, the risen Jesus no longer belonged to quite the same reality in which they had known him before the crucifixion. The risen Jesus comes and goes mysteriously; he is difficult to recognize; he is not to be limited to some particular place or time. Yet, when people (most of them already his disciples) did encounter him, they were sure that, however hard he was to recognize at first, it was truly Jesus whom they had met.

The challenge to the proclaimer of Jesus' resurrection, then as now, was to speak of this event in such way as to reveal to the hearer that it is not merely an oddity or a singularity—much less a fiction—but an opening onto a more profound dimension of reality, a dimension that embodies the same, startling good news that was already at the heart of Jesus' life and message. This is the challenge that faced the writers of the Gospels as much as their heirs who preach the resurrection from pulpits on Easter Day in the modern world.

GOSPEL: JOHN 20:1-18; LUKE 24:1-12

The lectionaries are almost evenly divided between two Gospel readings for Easter morning: John's account of Mary Magdalene in the garden (appropriate to the overall Johannine orientation of the Eastertide lectionary) and Luke's account of the women encountering the angel at the tomb (related to the use of Luke elsewhere in year C). These are primarily accounts of the finding of the empty tomb. Only the longer version of the Johannine reading (20:1-18) includes an encounter with the Risen Lord.

Luke 24:1-12. Luke's account of the finding of the empty tomb follows directly on the burial of Jesus by Joseph of Arimathea, who wrapped the body in fine linen (there is no mention of any spices). The women who had followed Jesus from Galilee observed what Joseph did and prepared fragrances and myrrh to complete the proper burial after the sabbath. Luke continues, without any break and with a simple pronoun, "they," to tell of the women's arrival at the tomb on Sunday morning. Their expectations are completely defeated when they find the tomb standing open and no corpse inside it. They are "at a loss" (v. 4), and it is precisely while they are in this state of disorientation that the "two men" appear before them.

This state of disorientation, in one form or another, is typical of the resurrection narratives. It arises from the confounding of normal expectations. Far from trying to slip past this difficulty in coming to terms with the resurrection, the Gospel writers emphasize it. They treat it as an essential aspect of the encounter with the risen Christ.

The women recognize the two male figures as angels by their clothing, which flashes like lightning—a nuance of the Greek difficult to convey in English translations. Their reaction to these figures of power embodies both fear and reverence. Such visitations, however much accepted in first-century Jewish culture, were rare and disturbing; they signal a break with everyday reality, not a continuation of it.

Yet, the angels remind the women of Jesus' prediction of his passion, death, and resurrection. The angels thus speak not by their own authority, significant though it was, but by the authority of Jesus. They imply that the women could have known what to expect, could have had their normal expectations already shaken and reshaped by Jesus' teaching. One may even hear a hint of reproof in "Why are you seeking the living one among the dead? He is not here, but has been raised" (vv. 5-6). The disorientation brought about by the resurrection of Jesus is continuous with the disorientation brought about by his teaching.

The women return to the larger Christian community to be the first bearers of the good news of the resurrection. The reading ends here in the *BCP* lectionary, but those using it would do well to exercise the rubrical permission to lengthen lessons, for the simple proclamation by the women of their good news is not the whole story. The doubt of the others is equally important—underlining that the event, even if consonant with Jesus' teaching, was still profoundly unexpected.

The earliest Christians no doubt had to respond to charges of gullibility. Telling of the disciples' initial doubt and hesitation may have helped to reassert their credibility as witnesses. At the same time, there are profound spiritual reasons for this emphasis. One purpose is to acknowledge the impossibility of the message itself. To believe in the resurrection is not to accept the obvious, but rather to affirm something impossible as truer to one's actual experience than what is normal and predictable. Belief in the resurrection involves conversion. The repeated doubt of the earliest witnesses makes exactly this point.

Another significant point is the marginality of the first witnesses. The Gospel accounts agree that the earliest witnesses to the resurrection, whether discovering the empty tomb or even (according to Matthew and John) first meeting the risen Lord, were marginal people, people of no legal account—women, to be precise. Since it was scarcely advantageous to the earliest Christians to repeat this aspect of the story, its preservation must be credited to their strong sense that the gospel is particularly accessible to the poor and marginalized. This is, in fact, another aspect of the disorientation that characterizes the resurrection. In the moment of the resurrection, the last become first, those commonly thought of as least equipped to understand the mystery are those who find it easiest to grapple with.

John 20:1-18. The reading from the Fourth Gospel exemplifies many of these same motifs. The shorter version of the reading contains only the story of Mary Magdalene's discovery of the empty tomb. The general drift is much the same as in Luke's version, but there are significant differences. Mary comes to the tomb alone, it seems, and while it is still dark. Given the importance of darkness-light dualism in John, it is not difficult to see this as suggesting her ignorance of the true state of affairs at the tomb.

As in Luke's account, the discovery that the stone is gone is profoundly disturbing and disorienting. Mary runs to take counsel with Peter and the Beloved Disciple. The way she describes the situation makes it clear that she thinks Jesus is still dead and the problem is a missing corpse: "They have taken the Lord out of the tomb, and we don't know where they've put him" (20:2). Peter and the Beloved Disciple run to the tomb to see for themselves. Peter even barges into the unclean space (something neither Mary nor the Beloved Disciple was prepared to do) and finds clear evidence of a body having been unwrapped, but nothing more.

The Beloved Disciple follows Peter into the tomb and it is then said that "he saw and believed" (20:8). But what does that mean? "To believe" (*pisteuo*) is a positive word for John—but not unambiguously so. It is quite possible for people to believe and yet not be trustworthy (2:24) or to

THE RESURRECTION OF OUR LORD—EASTER DAY

believe and then fall away over a hard saying (6:60-66). And, later on, Jesus will say to Thomas that it is those who have *not* seen and yet have believed who are blessed (20:29).

John goes on to note that "they did not yet know the scripture that he must rise from the dead" (20:9). What the Beloved Disciple seems to have "believed" on his visit to the tomb is simply that it was empty—but in a perplexing way. Whoever took the body had gone to the trouble of unwrapping it, taking it away naked, leaving behind the valuable winding-cloth (textiles were relatively more costly in antiquity than today). One is reminded, too, that Lazarus, when Jesus raised him from the dead, needed to be helped out of his grave-clothes, which are described in much the same terms as those used here (11:44).

Even with all these hints—and despite the fact that John's Christian audience already knew the rest of the story—the account is curiously inconclusive. We are left with *belief* that the tomb was empty—something disorienting in its own right—but not yet with any real recognition of the resurrection. The lectionaries that conclude the reading here may perhaps have made an error in judgment, for the Johannine account of the finding of the empty tomb is not a complete narrative in its own right like those of the Synoptic evangelists.

If, with the Revised Common Lectionary, we follow the story through to its conclusion, we remain at the tomb with Mary Magdalene, who is faithful in and to her sorrow. Nothing can distract her from the depth of her grief, which is, after all, the normal response to the loss of the beloved. She is living, still, in the preresurrection world, the world that will not and cannot imagine something so unthinkable. Even when she looks into the tomb and sees angels sitting there, the strangeness of their presence does not seem to register with her. A corpse, according to the Torah, would generate the most radically contagious sort of uncleanness (Num. 19:11-22). Yet, here are two members of the heavenly court taking their ease in a tomb!

Even when the angels ask Mary a question, she refuses to allow them to distract her from her grief. She does not so much as ask if they know where the body is. Only when she sees a human being who might be responsible for the garden around the tomb does she ask that question. She looks at this person, yet does not recognize him as Jesus. Recognition takes place only when Jesus calls her by name. One is reminded of how Jesus calls Lazarus out of the tomb by name (11:43) and of Jesus' saying about the Good Shepherd who calls his sheep by name (10:3).

In short, the power to make sense of the resurrection does not lie with the observer, but only with the resurrected one. Only when Jesus names Mary can she recognize who he is. And with that recognition comes conversion:

She finds her entire world turned around and so becomes the first proclaimer of the good news of the resurrection, which is not just a piece of information but a new way of construing the world.

Even so, Jesus remains beyond Mary's grasp. He is not to be hung onto, as he ascends to the Father and completes his crossing over into the One from whom he came (cf. 13:1). The resurrection of Jesus can be proclaimed, but not possessed. It can never become a comfortable part of our world, our sense of everyday reality. It remains always absurd and unthinkable, however true.

SECOND LESSON: 1 CORINTHIANS 5:6-8; 15:1-11, 19-26; COLOSSIANS 3:1-4

To complement the Gospel readings, the lectionaries have turned to a variety of sources. The Revised Common Lectionary draws from *1 Corinthians 15:19-26*, Paul's great defense of the general resurrection. In the passage chosen, Paul asserts that Jesus' resurrection is only the beginning of a world-historical process that will culminate in the restoration of God's sovereignty over the whole creation. This will involve the resurrection of the faithful at Christ's appearing (15:23) and the nullification of all subordinate powers and authorities that may have come between God and God's world and introduced their own purposes and interests into the governance of God's creation (15:24).

The resurrection of Jesus turns out to be a revolutionary act—as revolutionary as Adam's rebellion, which introduced death into the world. It will reach its ultimate, revolutionary goal when it gives life to all (15:22). Later Christians have sometimes used the doctrine of resurrection to palliate oppression in this world—the teaching of "pie in the sky by and by." But the doctrine of resurrection is not simply about the last day. The truth of the resurrection begins now. It begins at the moment one becomes aware of it, the moment of conversion. From that moment, as Paul asserts elsewhere in 1 Corinthians 15, one becomes a citizen of the age to come, a citizen of the resurrection, and begins to live according to the resurrection, not according to the slavery of human notions.

The relation between Christ's resurrection and present Christian conduct is even clearer in *Colossians 3:1-4*. Christians have already been "raised with Christ" (in baptism). Their conduct is governed by the values of the age to come, where "your life is hidden with Christ in God." The truest human existence is a life of peace and justice lived in close communion with God and with other human beings. Christians are to live such a life, "the things above," even now. Indeed, we begin to understand who we truly are only as we begin to see ourselves transformed in the resurrection. "When Christ, your life, is manifested, then you, too, will be manifested along with him in glory." Before that moment, we have only a dim, though growing, notion of who we are. As we focus our present life on the life of the resurrection, our humanity moves toward its true goal.

Yet another option for the epistle reading is *1 Corinthians 5:6-8*, a brief text that describes Christian life as a Passover festival in the light of Jesus' sacrificial death. For a fuller treatment of this passage, see the discussion of the readings for Easter Evening or Easter Monday below.

The *LBW* choice is Paul's recitation of the oral tradition he had received about Jesus' resurrection in *1 Corinthians 15:1-11*. While it is interesting to have this standing alongside the materials in the Gospel reading, perhaps its greatest value is that Paul includes his own experience of the risen Lord in the list, thus suggesting that the encounter with the risen Jesus is by no means confined to a short list of events on and immediately after the first Easter Day.

FIRST LESSON: ACTS 10:34-43; ISAIAH 65:17-25; 51:9-11; EXODUS 15:1-11; PSALM 118:14-24

Most of the lectionaries agree in using some part of Peter's speech to the household of Cornelius as the first lesson (*Acts 10:34-43*). The speech briefly recounts the story of Jesus' ministry, culminating with resurrection appearances "not to the whole people but to the witnesses selected beforehand by God." The resurrection of Jesus thus leads to proclamation by means of personal interaction with him ("we ate with him and drank with him after his resurrection from the dead"). In keeping with the element of conversion implied by the encounter with the risen Jesus in the Gospels, the continuation of Jesus' message is entrusted only to those who have been shaped by their experience of him.

The shorter version of this reading in the Roman Catholic lectionary loses Peter's opening acknowledgment that the good news of the resurrection transcends normal human and religious divisions. For Easter Sunday itself, the loss is minor, but the omitted verses would help set the stage for the readings from Acts that will follow during Eastertide.

The lectionaries offer some alternative first readings from the Scriptures of Israel. *Isaiah 65:17-25* offers an image of an earthly paradise, a picture of ideal human existence. Understood as a metaphor of the age to come, it reflects not merely physical well-being—a world with plenty to eat and drink, a world without premature death—but also a world of justice and peace. There will be no more war or theft. The peace of that world will transform the whole created order so that the lion eats straw like the ox. It is a vivid image of a world that will allow for full expression of the goodness of our created humanity. It is the world of which Christians are already citizens, already being transformed according to its truth.

Isaiah 51:9-11 is a brief, celebratory evocation of God's triumph over chaos and death. The Rahab of v. 9 is the chaos monster of that name, not the Canaanite woman whom Matthew lists as an ancestor of Jesus (1:5). This and the implicit identification of the sea with chaos and death may require some explanation if the passage is to be meaningful to the modern audience.

Exodus 15:1-11 (The First Song of Moses) is an appropriate lesson in the way that it links with the themes of the Easter Vigil, but perhaps a bit bloodthirsty for Easter morning. Its alternative, *Psalm 118:14-24*, has fewer drawbacks.

Easter Evening or Easter Monday
The Resurrection of Our Lord

Lectionary	First Lesson	Psalm	Second Lesson	Gospel
Revised Common	Isa. 25:6-9	Psalm 114	1 Cor. 5:6b-8	Luke 24:13-49
Episcopal (BCP)	Acts 5:29a, 30-32 or Dan. 12:1-3	Psalm 114 or 136 or 118:14-17, 22-24	1 Cor. 5:6b-8 or Acts 5:29a, 30-32	Luke 24:13-35
Roman Catholic	Acts 2:14, 22-32			Matt. 28:8-15
Lutheran (LBW)	Dan. 12:1c-3 or Jon. 2:2-9	Psalm 150	1 Cor. 5:6-8	Luke 24:13-49

GOSPEL: LUKE 24:13-49; MATTHEW 28:8-15

Luke 24:13-49. As we noted above, most of the Gospel readings chosen for Easter morning include only the finding of the empty tomb, without any resurrection appearances. That changes on Easter Evening, when resurrection appearances dominate. Most of the lectionaries choose Luke's Emmaus narrative for this purpose (24:13-35), with or without the following appearance in Jerusalem (vv. 36-49). These narratives continue to exemplify the characteristics of resurrection narratives noted in relation to the Easter morning Gospel readings. It is indeed Jesus whom the disciples encounter, but he proves elusive—difficult to recognize and no longer defined by the familiar everyday world of the here and now.

The resurrection cannot be caught in the expectations of the familiar world. Its importance is precisely that it breaks those expectations apart so that one is opened to the possibility of a new relationship with God, the world, one's neighbor, and oneself. In this way, it works rather like Jesus' parables, which often present some startlingly unexpected element in an otherwise familiar framework in order to defeat our expectations and open up new possibilities.

Language about resurrection, like language about God, is inherently metaphorical in character. It points us beyond the confines of ordinary human knowledge, beyond the things for which we have ready-made vocabulary, and shadows forth the inexpressible. The resurrection of Jesus intersects history in the form of the empty tomb, yet it is not primarily a historical event but rather a transcendent movement, a step into the life of the age to come. As such, it is a step that carries Jesus beyond our immediate grasp, but not beyond glimpse—not, at least, if he deigns to signal to us.

Hence the persistent motif in the resurrection appearances that shows Jesus as taking the initiative to make himself known and so overcome the unwillingness, ignorance, or thick-headedness of the disciples. In John's Gospel, he addresses Mary Magdalene by name—and only then becomes recognizable (20:16). In Luke's Emmaus story, he walks with the two disciples and explains Scripture to them, but becomes known only in the moment of blessing and breaking bread with them (24:30-31). At the subsequent appearance in Jerusalem, the gathered disciples at first think they are seeing a ghost and react with fright; only by asking for a piece of fish and eating it before them does Jesus persuade them that it is indeed he (24:36-42).

The resurrection comes to seem possible only after experiencing it, which results in conversion to belief in the God who has in fact raised Jesus and so to a notion of the world as a place where this has happened and can happen. It cannot be known in advance. The early Christians looked back on it as something prefigured in Jesus' teaching, but not knowable until it had taken place. While the explicit predictions of the resurrection in the Gospels may well have been postresurrection churchly formations read back into the tradition of Jesus' own teachings, it remains true that Jesus' resurrection was deeply in accord with his teaching about God as lover, forgiver, reclaimer, renewer.

Having experienced the power of God in Jesus' ministry and resurrection, the early Christians then returned to their Scriptures (that is, the Scriptures of Israel, for the most part in the Old Greek version) and found that they took on new meaning. The center of Scripture lay not in its legal authority, but in the way it looked forward to a renewal of God's relationship with Israel (and, ultimately, all humanity) in the person of Christ. Jesus' opening of Scripture to the Emmaus travelers follows the pattern of early Christian biblical interpretation itself. When they came to understand the Scriptures as speaking about Jesus' ministry and the power of the resurrection, they found them full of hitherto unsuspected meaning.

The fact that Jesus becomes known to the Emmaus disciples precisely at the moment of breaking bread points both backward in Luke's narrative to Jesus' practice of eating with the disciples and others (for instance, Zacchaeus, 19:1-10) and forward to the common meal of the Christian churches, which eventually becomes the Eucharist. There are familiar moments in our Christian experience that can serve as windows on the reality of the resurrection. However impossible the resurrection itself may seem, it breaks in on us at moments when our guard is down and we are open to sharing with others and therefore to sharing a reality that is larger than our own.

Another aspect of the Emmaus narrative has also come to be of interest recently—namely, the relationship of the two travelers. Since they can invite Jesus to stay with them, it appears that they are members of the same household and live at Emmaus. It is possible to think of them as a married couple, acting jointly as Jesus' hosts. Given the paucity of such figures in the Gospels, many modern readers will welcome this possibility. It may also be noted that the pronouns that refer to this pair are masculine in gender. In the rules of ancient Greek grammar, this is consistent with their being one male and one female; but it is also possible to read them as both male. It may, then, be possible that this is a household composed of two men. From Luke's perspective, all this was probably incidental to his own purpose in telling the story, and we cannot be certain what picture he had in mind.

The Jerusalem appearance (24:36-49) will be found to reiterate the same points mentioned above about the relationship, for early Christians, between Jesus and Scripture. It is Jesus' life and teaching that interprets the Scriptures more than the other way round. Moreover, this new understanding of Scripture leads to a proclamation of "conversion for the remission of sins to all the nations" (that is, the Gentiles). Once again, according to Luke, Jesus predicts something that will be hard to recognize or accept when it actually occurs. Just as the resurrection itself was hard to imagine until after it had happened, so, too, the bringing of Gentiles into the Christian community will be subject to great controversy, despite the fact that Luke's Jesus has already predicted it in this resurrection appearance.

Matthew 28:8-15. The Roman Catholic lectionary assigns a different Gospel for this evening, Matthew 28:8-15, which begins with the story of Jesus' appearance to the women who have just left the tomb after finding it empty. This is a very brief narrative, but it squares with the main elements noted previously. Jesus takes the initiative by greeting the women. They confirm his reality for the reader by taking hold of his feet (a normal suppliant gesture of the time). And their encounter with the risen Jesus makes them witnesses and messengers to the male disciples.

The reading continues with the account of the guards' flight into the city of Jerusalem where they are suborned by the authorities with bribes and a guarantee of immunity. Matthew may well have included this story in response to contemporary rumors, but it also plays a spiritually appropriate role in the larger Easter story. We have already stressed the difficulty, even for the believer, of accepting the reality of the resurrection and how it requires a conversion before one can see the world in the light of this reality. The story of the guards reveals the determination of the world (something the believer is still involved in, too) to protect itself from such notions. The world is committed to the myth of its own self-sufficiency and is willing to believe a lie in order to protect it.

SECOND LESSON: I CORINTHIANS 5:6-8

All the lectionaries that provide an epistle for Easter Evening agree in choosing 1 Cor. 5:6[6b]-8. This passage takes the practice of clearing leaven out of the house before Passover as an image of the transformed life of the believer—transformed into "the unleavened bread of sincerity and truth." The text reaffirms the fact that Easter is not merely a question of formal belief, but implies a true conversion, including transformation of life. Sincerity and truth are fundamental qualities of such a life. The Jesus of the Synoptic Gospels (Matthew, Mark, and Luke) treats hypocrisy as the most fundamental sin; the Jesus of John's Gospel emphasizes truth as a fundamental mode of connection with God.

The reference to Jesus as our Passover *sacrifice* may make most modern hearers think more of Good Friday than of Easter. It is important to remember, however, that the death of the victim, while an integral part of ancient sacrifice, did not exhaust the meaning of sacrifice. Most sacrifices (that of Passover included) culminated in a banquet that celebrated a renewed communion between the worshiper and the deity. The passage should probably be heard, then, in eucharistic terms. The bread of sincerity and truth is the life of the risen Jesus now shared with his followers.

FIRST LESSON: ISAIAH 25:6-9; DANIEL 12:1-3; JONAH 2:2-9; ACTS 2:14, 22-32; 5:29-32

The lectionaries offer a miscellaneous selection of first lessons. *Isaiah 25:6-9* contains the vision of a great eschatological banquet on Mt. Zion, when God "will swallow up death forever." It is an engaging choice for Easter, as it strikes a highly celebratory note and offers a chance to emphasize the connection of the resurrection of Jesus with the general resurrection at the last day.

Daniel 12:1-3 is less celebratory, including as it does a prophecy of tribulation. It does, however, introduce the larger apocalyptic picture that was the original context of ancient Jewish belief in the resurrection. And it contains the only unambiguous reference to resurrection in the Hebrew Bible.

Jonah 2:2-9, the Prayer of Jonah, contains imagery of being called back from Sheol. The selection may remind us of the popularity of Jonah iconograpy in early Christian art, where the fish vomiting up Jonah was a common symbol of resurrection.

The choice of passages from Acts in two of the lectionaries prefigures the use of Acts that will characterize the rest of Eastertide. The reading from *Acts 5:29a, 30-32* is a selection from Peter's speech to the Sanhedrin after the disciples have been told to stop teaching in the name of Jesus. It offers a brief recapitulation of the passion and resurrection tradition. In the truncated form chosen, however, it loses much of its force. The preacher who wishes to emphasize it may wish to read a longer version, including the authorities' complaint that the disciples "want to bring this man's blood on us" (5:28). In response, Peter says, in effect, "Well, you—the authorities—did kill him! But his death is for good to the whole people." Without some such expansion, the passage could actually be heard as a reiteration of the bizarre but long-standing libel that Jews generally were or are responsible for the death of Jesus.

The passage from *Acts 2:14, 22-32* is an excerpt from Peter's Pentecost speech, again offering a recapitulation of the passion and resurrection tradition. Again, it may be necessary (or, at least, wise) to offer some rebuttal to notions of Jewish responsibility for the death of Jesus. Peter accuses the specific persons in his audience of complicity in the death of Jesus—not their descendants, much less Jews in general.

Other hearers may be disturbed by the statement that the death of Jesus happened by "God's fixed will and foreknowledge" (v. 23). Language about the Father's sacrifice of the Son that once seemed routine in Christian speech is now being questioned as suggesting a radically abusive kind of relationship between parents and children. One must acknowledge that, rightly or wrongly, the ancient Mediterranean world saw children in a very different light from the modern West. It saw them more as extensions of their family, existing for the good of the family, than as individuals in their own right.

That said, however, one must still grapple with what Christians have really understood by such language. Jesus is not handed over as a mere instrument of God's purposes. Quite the contrary, the doctrines of the Trinity and incarnation hammered out in the fourth and fifth centuries serve above all to affirm that the sacrifice is a *self*-sacrifice on the part of God. Even without this full, later doctrinal apparatus, the New Testament writers were affirming that Jesus was intimately associated with God in this action.

In the context of Peter's speech, the point is that God can use an evil act to achieve a beneficent goal. One is reminded of Joseph's speech to his brothers: ". . . it was not you who sent me here, but God" (Gen. 45:8). The biblical writers tend to insist on a divine agency at work even in the most inauspicious of circumstances.

Second Sunday of Easter

Lectionary	First Lesson	Psalm	Second Lesson	Gospel
Revised Common	Acts 5:27-32	Ps. 118:14-29 or Psalm 150	Rev. 1:4-8	John 20:19-31
Episcopal (BCP)	Acts 5:12a, 17-22, 25-29 or Job 42:1-6	Psalm 111 or Ps. 118:14-29	Rev. 1:(1-8), 9-19 or Acts 5:12a, 17-22, 25-29	John 20:19-31
Roman Catholic	Acts 5:12-16	Ps. 118:1-4, 13-15, 22-24	Rev. 1:9-11a, 12-13, 17-19	John 20:19-31
Lutheran (LBW)	Acts 5:12, 17-32	Psalm 149	Rev. 1:4-18	John 20:19-31

GOSPEL: JOHN 20:19-31

The Gospel lection contains three somewhat independent elements: Jesus' appearance to the disciples on the evening of Easter Day and his giving of the Spirit; Jesus' appearance to the disciples and Thomas one week later; and a statement about John's purpose in writing the Gospel. These are interrelated, but have distinct points to make.

John treats the giving of the Spirit quite differently from Luke. Rather than separating it out as an event in its own right, inaugurating an "age of the church," as Luke has done, John links it very closely to Jesus and his "crossing over." Scholars have long observed that the Johannine tradition was not very interested in institutional matters. For John, the significance of the church lies less in itself than in the way it remains in continuity (and, indeed, unity) with Jesus himself.

The appearance on Easter evening (20:19-23) begins, in a way common to resurrection appearances, with an indication of discontinuity from ordinary experience: unexpectedly (and contrary to the normal rules of space and time), Jesus joins the disciples in a locked room. The disciples have locked themselves in "for fear of the Jews" (that is, of the authorities), who they think will pursue them as followers of a condemned and executed rebel. Jesus appears and greets them with "Peace to you." The significance of the greeting is twofold. It reminds the hearer of Jesus' claim at the Last Supper: "Peace I leave with you. My peace I give to you" (14:27). It also contrasts as sharply as possible with the anxiety that has made the disciples shut themselves in. While the disciples have to expect hostility from the world (15:18-19), they can still remain in the peace that Jesus alone can give.

We should say a word here about John's repeated use of the phrase "the Jews" to describe Jesus' opponents (as contrasted with references to "scribes," "Pharisees," and so forth in the Synoptic Gospels). This Johannine usage has had disastrous effects on Christian attitudes toward Jews and Judaism in the altered circumstances that have prevailed since the time when Christianity became a clearly distinct religion and even the dominant religion in the Western world. Preachers who are speaking from Johannine texts have an obligation to raise the issue of what this language did and did not mean in its own day in order to help prevent further harm to the nation to which both Jesus and John belonged.

To comprehend this language, we need to understand, with current scholarship, that the Johannine community was itself composed of Jewish Christians in the process of separating from the larger Jewish community. It may be helpful to compare the way the term *Catholic* functioned for Protestants and Anglicans after the Reformation. While most such groups continued to use the historical creeds and to profess belief in "one, holy, catholic, and apostolic church," popular usage tended to equate "Catholic" with "Roman Catholic" and even to use it as a term of abuse. Much the same process must have been at work in the Johannine community, Jewish as it was.

Returning to John's treatment of the resurrection appearance, we find that, as usual, Jesus takes the initiative in identifying himself. By showing his wounds, he authenticates his risen continuity with the person who taught, worked miracles, and died on the cross. Yet, he is also changed, as his appearance in the locked room indicates. He is a figure of power—a power that he will now share with his disciples in a particular way.

Jesus again addresses them with the phrase, "Peace to you." The repetition is not accidental, but a significant introduction to what follows. Just as we learn at the beginning of John's Gospel that all things flow from the Father by way of the Word (1:3-4), we are reminded again here that the stability and fruitfulness (the peace) of Christian life is a gift from God through Jesus. And it is the sharing of this gift that allows the disciples to carry on the original mission of Jesus in the world. Jesus sends his disciples out "just as" the Father had sent him.

The peace that Jesus gives is the foundation of this mission. The mission is not simply a duty to be undertaken out of obedience, but a gift to be shared by the power inherent in it. This is further expressed when Jesus breathes on the disciples, thus sharing with them "Holy Spirit/wind/ breath." This is a sharing of Jesus' own essence. (The later clarity about the identity of the Holy Spirit as the third person of the Trinity, enshrined in the version of the Nicene Creed approved at Constantinople in 381, is not to be found in John.) It also recalls the account of how God breathed life into the first human in Genesis 2 and so constitutes a kind of remaking of humanity in full communion with God.

The giving of the Spirit brings with it the power to release sins or to hold onto them. This verse has often been connected to the later Christian authority to perform sacramental absolution, usually restricted to the ordained. It is unlikely that any such notion was in John's thought-world. As I have already mentioned, the Johannine community seems to have been unusually indifferent to institutional issues—even by first-century Christian standards. And the group to whom the Spirit is given is simply "the disciples," by which John designates the whole community of the faithful, not some subgroup of leaders.

What, then, is this power given to the faithful to release or hold onto sins? It is probably impossible to make sense of the passage in any juridical way. If we are all judges, what do we do when we disagree? It refers rather to a power implicit in the Christian experience of God to share with others the power of God's forgiveness of sin, the fundamental truth of the gospel itself. The Christian who has experienced God's insistent forgiveness in her own case is uniquely able to share it with others. She can do so with the authority of her own experience. Our pronouncement of God's forgiveness depends on this personal certainty of it.

But what of the power to "hold onto sins" (giving it a very literal translation)? Unlike the Jesus of Mark and Matthew, John's Jesus never speaks of an unforgivable sin. Yet, he does acknowledge that some people may "die in their sins" (8:21). The difference lies not in God's refusal to forgive, but in our inability to grasp or accept that forgiveness. This is true, above all, of people who wrap themselves in religion as a defense against God. If Jesus suggests that his followers may "hold onto" the sins of some, it is not because he wishes to limit God's forgiveness in some way or to place some people beyond its reach. After all, John holds that Jesus came in order to save the world not to condemn it (3:17). But the power to give is not the power to force acceptance of the gift.

The following episode of Jesus' appearance to the disciples with Thomas explores some of these themes further. Thomas's initial refusal to believe is not merely skepticism, but a failure to grasp (or be grasped by) the unthinkable reality of the resurrection. Ultimately, he is one for whom seeing is believing. Initially, however, he demands more than that: He must touch the wounds before he will believe that this strange visitor is actually the Jesus whom he had known. He insists on exploring the mystery of the resurrection perhaps beyond the limit to which it can in fact be known. Remember that Mary was told not to "hold onto" (or perhaps even to touch) Jesus on Easter morning (20:17).

When Jesus does appear to the group in Thomas's presence, he does so as mysteriously and impossibly as before. Again, he greets them with

"Peace to you." Jesus invites Thomas to stick his hand into the wound in Jesus' side. But sight turns out to be enough. Thomas not only believes, but utters a confession that John believes is profoundly correct: "[You are] my Lord and my God." Thomas is thus given the privilege of concluding the Gospel of John (assuming that it originally ended with 20:31) with the same recognition that began it: "In the beginning was the Logos. And the Logos was with God and the Logos was God."

Yet, however correct Thomas's confession may be, Jesus' final word here is, "Happy are they who have not seen and have believed." We often perceive this saying as a criticism of Thomas, but it is not precisely that. The point is not that God prefers the people who do not need to see. The Greek word here is *makarioi*, meaning "blessed" in the sense of "happy" or, in ordinary English, "lucky, fortunate."

Those who must see in order to believe are not so fortunate as those who can believe on the basis of what they hear. The latter have an easier time of it, do not have to struggle so much or so long, can enter more directly into the new perspective demanded by the reality of the resurrection. Yet, the belief that comes by hearing is itself dependent on what others have seen. Thomas's insistence on seeing leads not simply to his own conversion, but to his stating of the reality of Jesus in words that are profoundly true but that no one has used up to this point in the Gospel of John. Thomas's more difficult faith thus affords a foundation for the easier faith of those who come after him.

The concluding verses of the reading (probably the concluding sentences to an early draft of the Gospel of John) serve to emphasize the initial dependency of our faith on the observation of others. "These things have been written that you may believe . . . and have life." The faith of one Christian becomes the foundation for the faith of another. Not that faith is merely a form of words to be passed on. Faith or, better, "believing" (for John does not use the noun *pistis*), is rather the process by which our perception of the world is radically reshaped in accordance with the resurrection.

SECOND LESSON: REVELATION 1:1-19

The second lessons for Eastertide in Year C are drawn from the Revelation of John, a work with a checkered history among Christians. In the third century, Dionysius of Alexandria questioned the apostolicity of its authorship. It was slow to gain full acceptance as part of the New Testament canon in the East. Luther had reservations about it. It scarcely figured at all in the lectionary of the first Book of Common Prayer. Yet, it exerts an enduring fascination, above all because of the vivid images that clothe its message. Its suitability for Eastertide arises especially from the prominence it gives to the figure of the risen Jesus, whether in human form or in that of the Lamb that was slain.

The lectionaries assign to this Sunday portions of the opening material of the book, including the salutation from John to the "seven churches that are in Asia" (a Roman province in what is now western Turkey) and the initial vision of the risen Jesus. The author greets the churches with grace and peace from God and from Jesus, whom he describes as, among other things, "witness" and "firstborn from the dead." Jesus' witness and his experience of death relate his experience to that of the faithful who will be martyred in the tribulation that John predicts. (The Greek term for "witness" is the etymological source of the English word *martyr*.) By his death, the risen Jesus has freed the faithful from their sins and constituted them as "a kingdom, priests to God." The author praises and celebrates him (1:6) not just for his divine or quasi-divine glory (Revelation is not particularly clear about its Christology), but for the transformation that his passion and resurrection has brought about in human existence.

A vision of the risen and glorified Jesus follows the salutation (1:9-19). The passage has great visual power. John first sees the seven golden candlesticks and only then becomes aware of the resplendent figure standing among them. The whole image glows with so much fire and light that it seems barely possible to distinguish details. Yet, the details are important as expressing the richness and the power of the figure, who can actually hold the stars in his hand. There is also an element of threat in the sword proceeding from the figure's mouth.

John falls down as if dead and has to be reassured by the touch of the figure's hand. The figure, who is never named, identifies himself as the risen Jesus by referring to his experience of passion and resurrection: "I became dead and, see! I am alive for ever and ever." This self-identification is crucial to the message of Revelation, giving hope to the faithful who are called to martyrdom, since they will be able to suffer in imitation of their risen and glorified Lord.

FIRST LESSON: ACTS 5:12-32; JOB 42:1-6

The lectionaries draw the first reading from Acts 5, but vary as to what aspect of the story they present. One takes the summary account of the many miracles worked by Peter and the other disciples. This passage suggests that the ministry of Jesus does not cease with the resurrection and ascension but rather continues through the ministry of his followers, which is still a locus of healing power and therefore still potentially disturbing to the order of society.

Other lectionaries stress this latter element of social disturbance, which elicits jealousy from the religious officialdom. The authorities imprison the disciples, but an angel releases them in the night and tells them to return to their provocative behavior of teaching in the Temple. The disruptive power of the resurrection proves to be not merely an accidental byproduct of faithful behavior but a deliberate stratagem for living the life of the age to come in the here and now. The lection then ends either with Peter's insistence that one must obey God rather than human beings or with his proclamation of the resurrection (compare above on the propers for Easter evening).

The *BCP* lectionary provides an alternative lesson from the conclusion of the book of Job (*Job 42:1-6*). Job's response to his overwhelming encounter with God in the whirlwind may be understood here as an acknowledgment of the ineffability of everything beyond ordinary experience, whether Job's encounter with God or the early Christians' disorienting and perplexing experience of the resurrection of Jesus. One can parallel Job's experience in some ways with that of "doubting" Thomas. Just as Thomas had to see in order to believe, we hear Job saying, "I had heard of you by the hearing of the ear, but now my eye sees you." But perhaps Job's "seeing" is really closer to that mystical union with God that is, for John, the goal of all Jesus' life and ministry.

Third Sunday of Easter

Lectionary	First Lesson	Psalm	Second Lesson	Gospel
Revised Common	Acts 9:1-6, (7-20)	Psalm 30	Rev. 5:11-14	John 21:1-19
Episcopal (BCP)	Acts 9:1-19a or Jer. 32:36-41	Psalm 33 or Ps. 33:1-11	Rev. 5:6-14 or Acts 9:1-19a	John 21:1-14
Roman Catholic	Acts 5:27b-32, 40b-41	Ps. 30:2, 4-6, 11-13	Rev. 5:11-14	John 21:1-19 or John 21:1-14
Lutheran (LBW)	Acts 9:1-20	Psalm 30	Rev. 5:11-14	John 21:1-14

GOSPEL: JOHN 21:1-19

The lectionaries agree in assigning portions of John 21 to this Sunday. The shorter version of the lection includes only the basic story of an appearance of Jesus on the shores of the Sea of Tiberias, as John calls it. The longer version adds the conversation between Jesus and Peter on the same occasion.

The basic story shares important features with other appearance narratives. Once again, Jesus appears unexpectedly and proves difficult to recognize. Even after the Beloved Disciple has realized who it is, there is at least a hint of ongoing uncertainty: "None of the disciples was so bold as to ask him, 'Who are you?'—knowing that it was the Lord" (v. 12). The odd phrasing of this statement suggests that the disciples were both certain and uncertain at the same time, as is appropriate when the impossible is happening before your own eyes.

The story's particular vividness of detail is matched elsewhere among the resurrection narratives only by the journey to Emmaus. The rather offhand fishing expedition, the unfamiliar man standing on the shore in the faint dawn light, the astonishing catch of precisely 153 large fish, the even more amazing fact that the net is not broken by its huge load, the charcoal fire on the beach, with fish and bread already set out for breakfast—all these details serve to create an unusually vivid impression of the reality of the event, even as the author works to maintain its elusive and mysterious qualities.

The author underlines (v. 14) that this was the third time Jesus had appeared to the disciples after his resurrection. Accordingly, it is not merely the first appearance that is attended by uncertainty. The uncertainty is intrinsic to any encounter with the risen Jesus. It is the consequence of looking out from a familiar world onto the still scarcely imaginable life of the age to come.

The repeated references to food—and specifically to fish—also seem significant. In the first (v. 5), Jesus asks the men in the boat if they have anything to eat. When they say they do not, he tells them where to cast their net (vv. 5-6). But when they come ashore, they find a fire already kindled and a fish on it and a loaf of bread (v. 9). Jesus then invites them to bring some of the fish they have just caught, presumably to add to the common stock for a meal (v. 12). Finally, Jesus calls them to breakfast and himself takes the bread and the fish (singular in Greek, presumably the one fish already on the coals) and shares it out to them (vv. 12-13).

The language here is reminiscent of the institution of the Lord's Supper in the Synoptic Gospels. While this narrative is not found in the Fourth Gospel, there are indications that John expected his audience to know such common traditions. The fish itself often represented Christ for early Christians. And perhaps our author also expected the readers to know the tradition about Jesus' having made his disciples "fishers of humanity" (Mark 1:17). (It has even been claimed that the number of fish in the net corresponds to ancient notions of the number of human nations, but this seems, in fact, to be an error.) Whatever may be the exact background here, the story tells of the uniting of Jesus' contribution to the meal with that of the disciples. But it is Jesus who guides the disciples to their own catch of fish, and it is from his own supplies that he actually feeds them. This accords with the basic Johannine assertion of the absolute priority of the Logos of God over all human endeavor.

The longer version of the Gospel lection continues with a conversation between Jesus and Peter. Jesus initiates it with the question, "Simon, son of John, do you love me more than these people?" The nuances of this question depend on the name and character of Peter as it has been developed earlier in John's Gospel. To begin with, the name: Jesus adds to Simon the name "Peter" ("rock") in 1:42, and from that point onward he is always called either "Simon Peter" or simply "Peter" until the present passage. When Jesus addresses him here as "Simon, son of John," it threatens to deprive him of his additional name "Peter."

Peter has given grounds for some sort of disciplinary action. To be sure, all the male disciples except for the Beloved One ran away after Jesus' arrest, but Peter complicated his offense by insisting beforehand on his own unique loyalty: "Why can I not follow you? I'll lay down my life for you." To this, Jesus responds ironically, "Will you lay down your life for me? Amen, amen, I tell you the cock won't crow before you deny me three times" (13:37-38). The prediction is fulfilled, of course, during Jesus' trial (18:17-18, 25-27).

In John's account of Easter morning, Peter rushes to the tomb and is the first to go inside and see for certain that it is empty except for the graveclothes. Unlike the Beloved Disciple, he is not said to have believed as a result (20:3-10). He does not figure as an individual in the first two resurrection appearances, but this third one is staged precisely by his seemingly irrelevant decision to go fishing. Does this oddly private and personal decision suggest a certain inability to come to grips with the significance of the resurrection? Peter is not quick to recognize that the man on the beach is Jesus. The resurrected Lord does not yet form a part of his normal picture of the world. Yet, when he learns who it is, he leaps impetuously into the water to go to him. And he finds the strength to haul ashore single-handedly a netful of fish that all hands together had barely been able to drag toward the bank (21:6, 8, 11).

All these contradictions of character come together in Peter's conversation with Jesus. Peter is singled out for the question "Do you love me more than these people?" Peter understands this as a reproach and refuses to compare himself with the others, replying simply, "Yes, Lord, you know that I hold you in affection" (21:16). The question and answer are repeated, with variations, three times, a point explicitly underlined by the author. The threefold repetition corresponds to Peter's threefold denial. And each exchange concludes with a charge to Peter to "pasture/shepherd my sheep/lambs." This directive turns the point of the conversation away from Peter's own internal history of failure and love outward into a ministry to Jesus' other followers. Despite Peter's tendency to self-importance, his reconciliation is not for his own sake, but for that of the larger Christian community.

The passage concludes with an obscure oracle regarding Peter's old age, which the author of the chapter interprets for us as a prophesy of Peter's death. Here, finally, is the death that Peter said he was ready for in chapter 13. And it involves the negation of his earlier activist and forceful character. Peter's character does not change immediately, however, as the following passage shows (21:20-23). There he tries to compare his prophesied fate with that of the Beloved Disciple and is warned away from such speculations.

While the whole passage has sometimes been read as a kind of authorization of Peter and of Petrine ministry, that seems unlikely. John is notoriously unimpressed by the Twelve and uninterested in any kind of organized church life. It is easier to read the passage as a rehabilitation of Peter that constitutes him as a resource for the larger community of the faithful. This is also a more useful reading for the preacher since it connects with the life of the hearers, whose spiritual maturation comes about at least partly through reconciliation with God after failure.

SECOND LESSON: REVELATION 5:11-14

The second lesson, Revelation 5:11-14, is a celebration of the risen Jesus under the image of the Lamb that was slain. The vivid language of the passage stresses the amazing volume of sound (a phenomenon less remarkable in our own era of loudspeaker systems). While the passage begins by stressing the angelic and other supernatural voices, it continues (v. 13) by adding in a full range of voices from the earth, the sea, and the regions under the earth. Given this author's general pessimism about the present age, it is interesting to find him including these voices in the praise of the Lamb, whose work seems to involve their judgment, destruction, and replacement.

The language is hymnic and fairly general. Its general drift is that the Lamb is being associated very closely with "the one who is seated on the throne," so that the divine attributes of power, riches, wisdom, and so forth can be ascribed to the Lamb (v. 12) and the voices can offer "blessing and honor and glory and power" to both God and the Lamb (v. 13). The risen Jesus belongs somehow on God's side of the line between the divine and the created order, though Revelation makes no effort to explain such a situation metaphysically.

What this brief lection does not offer is any explanation of the occasion of this celebratory outburst. The longer version in the *BCP* lectionary fills in the context, which is the moment when the Lamb takes the book with seven seals to open it. But even this lection is not long enough to make complete sense; for that, one would need to begin at the beginning of chapter 5. The longer lesson also includes a reference to the blood of the Lamb as having purchased "a kingdom and priests" out of every human group, which brings us back to the this-worldly consequences of the passion and resurrection.

FIRST LESSON: ACTS 9:1-20; 5:27b-32, 40b-41; JEREMIAH 32:36-41

Most of the lectionaries draw their first lesson from *Acts 9:1-20* or portions thereof: the calling of Saul (called "Paul" from Acts 13:9 onward). This is a particularly appropriate choice for Eastertide, as Paul himself seems to have regarded his experience as belonging in the sequence of resurrection appearances (1 Cor. 15:1-8). Luke also treats the story as critically importance in conveying the message of Acts, reporting it not once but three times (cf. Acts 22:3-21; 26:9-20). He gives it a kind of companion relationship with another significant revelatory experience in Acts—Peter's vision of the great sheet let down out of heaven and filled with all sorts of animals (10:1-23). Together, these provide divine authority for the difficult transition the first-century church made from being a purely Jewish community to being a mixed community of Jews and Gentiles.

Since Saul was a Pharisee, his objections to the Christian movement may have rested on his impression that the believers were indifferent to the requirements of purity. There is much in the tradition of Jesus' own teaching (for instance, Mark 7:1-23) to suggest that he regarded purity as problematic in relation to the gospel. Purity is, indeed, religiously ambivalent. On the one hand, the maintenance of purity affords the worshiper a daily way of expressing relatedness to God and of preparing the self physically and, one hopes, spiritually, to approach the holy. On the other hand, there is a standing temptation for the religious to assume that those who are outside the circle of purity are distanced from God or even displeasing to God. The devotion to purity can thus serve to draw a person toward God but also to erect barriers between the pure and the impure. Much of Jesus' ministry seems to have been devoted to knocking down such barriers within the Jewish nation. The church after the resurrection of Jesus had to confront the greatest of these barriers, the one between Jew and Gentile.

The calling of Saul worked a great reversal—and not simply in turning him from being a persecutor of the church to being an evangelist. The great reversal is that he went from being an advocate of purity to being a missionary to Gentiles, who were completely outside the normal realms of purity as prescribed in Torah. Since Gentiles did not abide by Torah rules of purity, they were more or less automatically unclean. They might not be culpable for this, since the rules had been given only to Israel, not to them. Yet, they remained unclean, impure, or dirty—and therefore unacceptable to God. They were forbidden all access to the Temple, on pain of death. And impurity being to some extent contagious, they might compromise the purity of Israelites.

The purpose of Saul's calling is revealed, in the story, not to him, but to Ananias: "This man is my choice vessel to carry my name before both nations [that is, Gentiles] and kings and sons of Israel" (9:15). The rest of Paul's ministry is implicit in this calling. It is a vocation to a particular ministry that in turn demands a profound conversion, for the Saul who must bear God's name before the Gentiles will have to come to terms with the reality that God has chosen to approach the very people who were forbidden

THIRD SUNDAY OF EASTER 31

to approach God. It is anachronistic to speak of Saul as being converted from Judaism to Christianity. He remained as Jewish ever. But there was a conversion, nonetheless. The religion of purity had to give way to a religion of grace.

(For the Roman Catholic lectionary's reading from Acts 5, see the commentary above, under the Second Sunday of Easter.)

In the reading from *Jeremiah 32:36-41*, the most striking feature is not simply that it promises a return from exile, but that this promise is given at the very moment when the city is about to fall into the hands of its besiegers "by the sword, by famine, and by pestilence" (32:36). There is a stark contrast between the reality of the present situation and the promise given for the future. This accords with the startling aspect of Easter: God is shown as habitually overturning the human tendency to extrapolate current trends and introducing the unpredictability of the gospel.

Fourth Sunday of Easter

Lectionary	First Lesson	Psalm	Second Lesson	Gospel
Revised Common	Acts 9:36-43	Psalm 23	Rev. 7:9-17	John 10:22-30
Episcopal (BCP)	Acts 13:15-16, 26-33, (34-39) or Num. 27:12-23	Psalm 100	Rev. 7:9-17 or Acts 13:15-16, 26-33, (34-39)	John 10:22-30
Roman Catholic	Acts 13:14, 43-52	Ps. 100:1-3, 5	Rev. 7:9, 14b-17	John 10:27-30
Lutheran (LBW)	Acts 13:15-16a, 26-33	Psalm 23	Rev. 7:9-17	John 10:22-30

GOSPEL: JOHN 10:22-30

The Gospel reading today honors this Sunday's traditional designation as "Good Shepherd Sunday" by drawing from Jesus' Good Shepherd discourses in John's Gospel. It is not the most familiar part of these discourses, nor is it likely to be most people's favorite, since it has a strong element of Johannine "dualism." The Roman Catholic lectionary, in fact, delimits the reading in a way that reduces or removes this element, leaving a very short lection indeed.

The central element of the lection is the affirmation "My sheep hear my voice, and I know them and they follow me, and I give them eternal life." The use of such shepherd imagery has its roots in ancient imagery for leadership or kingship (compare the lection from Numbers in the *BCP* lectionary or Agamemnon's title "shepherd of men" in the *Iliad*). Recognizing this does not eradicate the element of intimacy and personal knowledge in John's Shepherd. But it identifies a purpose to the Shepherd's work—that of maintaining life and peace. Just as the shepherd defends the flock from predators, the ruler defends the community from its foes.

Nothing will snatch the sheep from Jesus' hand because nothing can snatch them from the Father's hand. And Jesus goes on to clarify this claim by saying, "The Father and I are one." It is this claim, according to John, that will get him killed in the end. Even now, it nearly does so, as the bystanders are ready to stone him (10:31). And it forms the prelude to a very dense passage in which John's Jesus exegetes a Psalm verse as referring to himself. The exegesis is unintelligible to the audience within the Gospel, however, since they do not know that Jesus is the incarnate Logos or Word.

But what about the dualism of the lection in its fuller form? Why were many early Christians so interested in drawing a sharp line between

FOURTH SUNDAY OF EASTER 33

themselves as the true flock and the others, the nonbelievers, who were outside? And why credit the difference to what sounds like predestination? "You are not my sheep. My sheep hear my voice." The basic dichotomy, of course, was a given of their experience. Since membership in the earliest Christian communities was primarily by choice, not by birth, they were strongly conscious that some made this choice while others, with apparently the same reasons to make it, did not.

Surprisingly enough, the early believers did not usually credit their choice to their own moral, religious, or intellectual superiority. They attributed it rather to the work of the Spirit. They experienced Jesus as choosing them more than themselves as choosing Jesus (cf. John 15:16). But what of the others, who have not made this choice? The claim that they do not belong to Jesus' sheep is less an explanation than an acknowledgment of the mystery. This not-belonging, to be sure, is not morally neutral. The behavior of those outside Jesus' flock is understood elsewhere in John's Gospel to be characterized by "the lie," that is, by a false understanding of the relationship between the world and its creator. But how is one delivered from this lie? Only by grace.

The difficulty modern Christians find with the doctrine of predestination arises from taking it out of the realm of spirituality and into dogmatic theology. In the context of early Christian spirituality, predestination is an acknowledgment of God's gracious generosity to the believer. In the context of dogmatic theology, it becomes a grand scheme for dividing humanity into haves and have-nots. The transposition alters the original meaning out of all recognition.

Jesus' response to the original question, however, becomes much clearer in the light of this material. The question was, "How long will you keep us hanging? If you are the anointed one, tell us openly." Jesus insists that he has already told them, though he has not in fact done so in any literal sense. His works are enough to identify him to any one capable of understanding who he is. Such persons belong to his sheep. Those who do not belong to his sheep will not understand even if he uses plain words—something he will in fact do at the end of the lection when he says, "I and the Father are one." Ultimately, then, Jesus refuses to engage with them in terms of their existing presuppositions. Only as those presuppositions change can they understand who he is.

The elusiveness of Jesus' identity here echoes the elusiveness of the resurrection appearances. Jesus cannot be grasped. Jesus cannot even be recognized except by some gift of grace. Indeed, to recognize Jesus involves a transformation of the person who recognizes: from the mourning Magdalene to the proclaimer of the resurrection, from the confused travelers to

Emmaus to the confident bearers of good news hurrying back to Jerusalem, from the doubting Thomas to the Thomas who confesses Jesus as Lord and God, from the failed and shamed Peter to the Peter who will testify to Jesus through martyrdom.

SECOND LESSON: REVELATION 7:9-17

The lection from Revelation contains more hymnic materials suitable to Eastertide, but its main interest is in the great multitude, clothed in white robes and holding palm branches. They are at least predominantly Gentiles, in contrast to the 144,000 Israelites enumerated in the preceding verses. But their major characteristic is not their ethnicity but the fact that they have suffered for their faith. They have come "out of the great tribulation" and have washed their robes "in the blood of the Lamb."

The period of unimaginable suffering called "the tribulation" is a common feature of apocalyptic eschatology in antiquity. It comes as the old world is descending into the ever-tightening control of evil and just before the divine intervention that brings the old world to an end and replaces it with the age to come. When the elder interprets the sufferings of Christians in terms of the tribulation, he is also, in effect, promising that the moment of divine intervention is close at hand.

Yet, there is also a shift in eschatology discernible here. The earliest Christian eschatology that we know (1 Thess. 4:13-18) speaks of the dead as sleeping until the moment of Christ's appearing, when there will be a general resurrection, followed by catching up those left alive into the air. Revelation is following a slighter newer tendency rooted in the experience of martyrdom, which held that the martyrs go directly to be with Jesus in heaven. There, no further harm can befall them. Their tears are dried, and they participate in the heavenly worship, singing praises to God and to the Lamb.

The idea of whitening robes in the blood of the Lamb may well refer in part to baptism, which could be understood both in terms of washing (1 Peter 3:21) and in terms of sharing in Christ's death (Rom. 6:3). But it also refers to the experience of martyrdom, as the following verses, with their references to tribulation and the reversal of all suffering, show. In this way, the lection emphasizes that, through the hope of resurrection, death changes its meaning even now. The life of faithfulness here is continuous with the life of the resurrection, being transformed already by the experience of Jesus.

FIRST LESSON: ACTS 13:14-16, 26-39, 43-52; 9:36-43; NUMBERS 27:12-23

The various lections from Acts fall out of step with one another at this point. Three of the lectionaries choose elements from the visit of Paul and Barnabas to Pisidian Antioch (*Acts 13*). Luke treats this episode as a kind of type-scene for Paul's ministry, much as he reworked the episode at Nazareth to provide an introductory scene for the ministry of Jesus (Luke 4:16-30). It begins with Paul and Barnabas being welcomed into the Jewish community and invited to speak in the synagogue. Paul's message attracts many, both in the Jewish community and in its halo of Gentile "God-fearers," people who have accepted much of the Jewish belief, but not, for the most part, actually converted to Judaism (such conversion, after all, was a change not only of belief but of nationality). But, in fairly short order, the new message leads to a division within the Jewish community, and the leaders of the community endeavor to stop its spread by disciplining the messengers. The result is a community of Christian believers, Jewish and Gentile, who are still tenuously related to the synagogue, but are now more specifically identified by their shared belief in Jesus.

The choice of the resurrection segment of Paul's speech is obviously appropriate to Eastertide, but may not add a great deal to what the congregation has already heard on this subject by now. The Christology implied in the speech, as usual in Luke, is lower than that implied in the Gospel of John. Paul speaks here of the resurrection as the moment of Jesus' adoption as God's Son.

Instead of Paul's speech, the Roman Catholic lectionary has chosen the end of the narrative, which involves a falling out with the local Jewish authorities (called, in rather Johannine vein, "the Jews"). Paul announces his intention to go to the Gentiles instead. This, of course, is a basic and repeated movement throughout Acts, underlined in the work's closing episode (28:28). In this particular case, Luke blames the shift on the jealousy of the local Jewish authorities, who fear that the popularity of the new message is undermining their own prestige. Luke recognizes that the arrival of the gospel did indeed have a destabilizing effect on society and, in this case, he confirms it by adding that the Jewish authorities were able to gain the support of prominent local citizens in expelling the missionaries.

There is also, once again, an element of predestination involved in interpreting the conversions: "as many as were appointed for eternal life believed" (v. 48). Compare the discussion of predestination above in relation to the Gospel for this Sunday. Both Luke and Paul seem to have maintained a hope that the predestined alienation of some would be temporary and they did not believe that anxiety over it should be allowed to interfere with the Gentile mission. Compare Paul's treatment of the topic in Romans 9–11.

The Revised Common Lectionary makes a quite different choice for the reading from Acts: the story of the raising of Tabitha (*Acts 9:36-43*). This is a welcome move, given the general tendency of the lectionaries to overlook stories involving women. It is also welcome for the other Eastertide motifs that it brings to the fore. Tabitha is herself an example of Christian life, already exhibiting the characteristic generosity of the life of the age to come. Her restoration to life shows that the power that was at work in the ministry of Jesus and in her work is also at work in the life of the believing community. When Luke brings the widows of Joppa on stage, weeping and showing Peter the clothes Tabitha had made while she was alive, it is not merely a heightening of pathos but a way of showing how the power of life had been at work in her.

The reading from *Numbers 27:12-23* portrays Jesus' namesake, Joshua, as shepherd of Israel (27:17, 21). It also deals with the issue of the transfer of power between generations. Moses is about to die without entering the Promised Land. Unless his authority is passed on in an orderly way, the people will be left in chaos. Yet, the new leadership must share characteristics of the old, in this case its constant communication with God. There is a broad parallel between this and the process Luke is presenting in Acts, the process by which the ministry of Jesus continues in that of the church.

Fifth Sunday of Easter

Lectionary	First Lesson	Psalm	Second Lesson	Gospel
Revised Common	Acts 11:1-18	Psalm 148	Rev. 21:1-6	John 13:31-35
Episcopal (BCP)	Acts 13:44-52 or Lev. 19:1-2, 9-18	Psalm 145 or Ps. 145:1-9	Rev. 19:1, 4-9 or Acts 13:44-52	John 13:31-35
Roman Catholic	Acts 14:21b-27	Ps. 145:1, 8-13	Rev. 21:1-5a	John 13:31-33a, 34-35
Lutheran (LBW)	Acts 13:44-52	Ps. 145:1-13	Rev. 21:1-5	John 13:31-35

GOSPEL: JOHN 13:31-35

The Gospel lection for this Sunday is the giving of the New Commandment. It comes from the beginning of the Last Supper discourses; indeed, it begins by referring to the departure of Judas, a vivid reminder that Jesus is on his way to the cross. Yet, Jesus speaks of this, in typically Johannine fashion, as a process of glorification that has already, in effect, taken place: "Now has the son of humanity been glorified. . . ." This process of glorification will move through the cross and resurrection and ascension until it achieves a complete "crossing over" into God (13:1). Hence the strange conjunction of tenses, past and future, here: "The son of humanity has been glorified. . . . And God will glorify him."

But what is this "glory"? The basic meaning of the Greek word *doxa* is "reputation"—public reputation that bestows honor. At the same time, however, *doxa* had also come to represent, for early Judaism and Christianity, the Hebrew idea of God's *shekinah*, the beauty and splendor of God's presence. In John, both ideas are operative. Jesus speaks of mutual love as the means by which people will recognize his disciples; public reputation is at issue. Yet, at the same time, the glory that the son of humanity shares with God is a glory from before the creation of the world (17:5); it is not dependent on acknowledgment by other creatures.

The emphasis on glorification in vv. 31-32 is pleonastic. The repetition goes beyond any necessity for making the idea clear and serves to drum the theme of glory into the hearer's mind as the key issue here. This done, John's Jesus goes on to indicate that this glory is beyond any human being's ability to attain. This puts the disciples and "the Jews" on an equal footing—a useful reminder to Christians who may feel that the Gospel of John guarantees them higher status or greater insight. What "the Jews" could not do, the disciples cannot do, either: follow Jesus through his glorification as he returns to the Father. The disciples will confirm their inability in the last

37

supper discourses when they prove not to understand Jesus' language about the path and the destination (14:1-11).

In a sense, Jesus has shown them the path already by giving them the new commandment to love one another. This differs from the summary of the Law we find in the Synoptic Gospels (Mark 12:28-34 and parallels). It is not, for one thing, composed of quotations from the Scriptures of Israel. For another thing, it focuses on the life of the Christian community in a way that the command to love one's neighbor as oneself does not. This can be read as backing away from the larger duty toward humanity that the summary of the Law entails, a kind of retreat into the community of the like-minded. Such a retreat would have been understandable for the Johannine communities in light of their persecuted status. Yet, I think something else is going on.

The point of the new commandment is not so much that the love of Christians is limited to their immediate fellowship but that one finds in the community a place where such love can and does blossom, where it becomes not only an individual act but a manner of life. As such, it becomes evidence for the connection of the church with Jesus and with Jesus' Father. The divine love that led to the creation and that seeks to call the creatures back from their self-absorption into relationship with the Creator—this love is the animating force of the community of the faithful.

The commandment brings with it, of course, a paradoxical demand. Only God can supply this love to the community, and yet the community is commanded to live by it and from it. Insofar as the community does so, it deserves no credit, since it is simply availing itself of divine gifts. Insofar as it rejects this love, it has fallen short of the glory that God has given it. The easy way in which Christians have sung "They will know we are Christians by our love" becomes problematic in this regard. It is problematic partly because Christians, past and present, are notable for hatred as well as love. It is also problematic because it seems to claim for the Christian community a kind of *possession* of this love as our own virtue. But in John's Gospel, the faithful have no such possessions, only gifts. It might be better to let others say, "We know you are Christians by your love," and to reply, "It is not ours. It is God's love for all creation, spread abroad among us."

SECOND LESSON: REVELATION 21:1-6; 19:1, 4-9

The reading from *Revelation 21:1-6* comprises the seer's vision of the new heaven and earth, with the new Jerusalem descending from heaven. The earliest conception of Jesus' resurrection saw it as a kind of firstfruits or down payment on the general resurrection in the last day. In the resurrection of

FIFTH SUNDAY OF EASTER 39

Jesus, the climax of the end time is bursting in on us. What could be more appropriate to Eastertide, then, than this passage celebrating the full gifts of the end time?

The new creation is significantly different from the old. The sea, that ancient symbol of the mysterious, ungovernable, chaotic element in our experience, is no more (v. 1). Along with it vanish death, mourning, crying, and hard labor (v. 4). What is left is a human life that will no longer be cut short before it reaches fullness and will no longer be characterized by conflict and suffering. These sentiments may have evoked a more intense reaction in a world without the relative conveniences and guarantees enjoyed by the Western middle classes of the current era, but they are still able to sound a meaningful note today. Indeed, we may all be able to face our griefs and losses more readily in light of this vision of a world where they have no further place.

Note, too, that this vision has a city at its heart—the new Jerusalem, described here, in language favored by mystics, as a bride adorned for her husband. Humanity will be united with God not one by one, but as a community. This is in the great biblical tradition that sees the age to come in social terms, beginning with the prophetic passage that describes it as a great feast on the mountain of God (Isaiah 25). Only something like the love-command in John's Gospel can make such a social vision of human existence credible or desireable.

The *BCP* lectionary uses a different reading, from *Revelation 19:1, 4-9*; but it also images the age to come in bridal terms, as the marriage supper of the Lamb. The identity of the bride with the called community is again clear, for she is adorned with "clean, bright linen," which is "the just actions of the saints." The lesson makes a jump to omit the verses rejoicing over the destruction of the bride's antitype—the great harlot. While the omission of such judgments seems appropriate to Eastertide, one can hardly avoid them altogether in dealing with Revelation. The sweetness and light of the new age are hard come by.

Because the life of the age to come involves the end of this age, in which human beings can hurt and destroy one another, we risk finding that we may not like it much. One can enter this scene of rejoicing only through a transformation of the self. This is made possible by grace, by the invitation to the supper of the Lamb, but it is still a process that must be experienced or even endured—one that is not always comfortable while it is happening. The beauty and delight of the age to come is daunting to whatever in us still harbors a grudge or aims at superiority over others or wants to dictate to others or exclude those who are different from ourselves. There is no heaven without personal and community transformation.

FIRST LESSON: ACTS 14:21b-27; 11:1-18; LEVITICUS 19:1-2, 9-18

The readings from Acts are again quite diverse. Two of the lectionaries have the passage from Acts 13 that concludes the episode at Pisidian Antioch. This has been discussed above, in relation to the Fourth Sunday of Easter.

The choice of the Roman Catholic lectionary (*Acts 14:21b-27*) serves much the same function as the passage from Acts 13 in that it signals the turn to the Gentiles. The reading is made up predominantly of dry itinerary, but it includes a reference to the regularizing of community life in the new churches through the appointment of elders (v. 23). And it concludes with Paul and Barnabas reporting to their home church "what God had done along with them and that he had opened to the Gentiles a door of faith" (v. 27). The turn to the Gentiles, of course, could not simply be a private undertaking on the part of Paul and his co-workers. It was critical to announce it and determine whether other Christians would support and accept the new converts.

The Revised Common Lectionary's choice of *Acts 11:1-18* works to the same end, but more effectively in that it contains Luke's most sustained argument for the inclusion of Gentiles as an expression of God's will. Peter here narrates his experience with the household of Cornelius for the benefit of critics who took exception to his having lodged and eaten with uncircumcised men (v. 3). Luke devotes a good deal of space to this rather detailed recitation, despite his having just finished the original narrative of the events (chapter 10). Given that this sort of repetition is not normal Lukan practice, one must conclude that Luke means to implant this material very emphatically in the mind and memory of the hearer.

The move to include Gentiles was the most difficult transition in the life of the first-century church, far more significant than doctrinal conflicts of the sort that would characterize second-century church life. Luke emphasizes Peter's vision, then, and the baptism of the household of Cornelius partly because they offer divine authority for this shift. And he shapes the narratives (both chapters 10 and 11) in such way as to emphasize that the Jewish-Christian community in Judea affirmed this innovation.

In chapter 10, Luke tells that other members of the Christian community at Joppa went with Peter (10:23) and consented to the baptisms (10:47). In chapter 11, "those of the circumcision" (that is, those who urged the necessity of circumcision for Gentile male converts) challenge Peter's action; but at the end of Peter's report, "They, when they heard these things, fell silent and glorified God, saying, 'Why, then, God has granted conversion even to the Gentiles'" (11:18).

Luke takes the acceptance of these first few Gentiles as establishing a precedent; and he will have Peter refer again to this experience at the Council of Jerusalem in Acts 15. When objections are raised there against the Gentile mission of Paul and Barnabas, Peter cites his experience to show that God had already shown a willingness to include Gentiles (15:6-11). Ultimately, the council reaffirms the legitimacy of the Gentile mission. This "break with tradition" is a story of particular significance in the late twentieth century, for it establishes the possibility of breaking with tradition as an element within the Christian tradition itself. Women, ethnic minority groups, and sexual minorities have all appealed to this element of revolution within the Christian tradition during this century, with the result that it has become central in a new way.

The lection from *Leviticus 19:1-2, 9-18* includes the second part of what goes to make up Jesus' summary of the Law: "You shall love your neighbor as yourself" (v. 18). This relates it indirectly to the love commandment in John's Gospel. Another link with the Gospel reading is the insistence of Leviticus that obedience to the commandment brings the worshiper close to God: "You shall be holy, for I the Lord your God am holy." In Leviticus, however, one key element of this "holiness" is purity of a physical, ritual kind, most elements of which were long ago left behind by Christians. Accordingly, the lesson omits verses referring to the correct eating of sacrifices (vv. 5-9), interbreeding of animals, sowing of different kinds of seed in the same field, mingling of fibers (v. 19), sex between a man and a slave woman (vv. 20-22), the "foreskin" of fruit trees (vv. 23-25), and so forth.

Since there is nothing to suggest that the authors of Leviticus regarded what we would call "moral" commandments as more important than the ones we might call "ritual," the passage raises important questions about selectivity in the use of Scripture, beginning with Jesus' own selectivity in choosing half of verse 18 as one of the two principal commandments in the Torah. Since the time of Jesus, Christians have always had to make decisions about the ongoing validity of specific elements in Scripture and tradition. The choice to admit Gentiles to the church was only the first major crisis of this sort.

Sixth Sunday of Easter

Lectionary	First Lesson	Psalm	Second Lesson	Gospel
Revised Common	Acts 16:9-15	Psalm 67	Rev. 21:10, 22—22:5	John 14:23-29 or 5:1-9
Episcopal (BCP)	Acts 14:8-18 or Joel 2:21-27	Psalm 67	Rev. 21:22—22:5 or Acts 14:8-18	John 14:23-29
Roman Catholic	Acts 15:1-2, 22-29	Ps. 67:2-6, 8	Rev. 21:10-14, 22-23	John 14:23-29
Lutheran (LBW)	Acts 14:8-18	Psalm 67	Rev. 21:10-14, 22-23	John 14:23-29

GOSPEL: JOHN 14:23-29; 5:1-9

John 14:23-29. The primary Gospel lection for the Sixth Sunday of Easter prepares the way for Ascension Day by speaking of the Spirit and its link to Jesus. The ascension will not mean the end of Jesus' ministry with the disciples, but only a shift of medium, for the Spirit, according to John, is closely associated with Jesus. The Spirit is *another* Paraclete or Sponsor (according to 1 John 2:1, Jesus is himself the principal Paraclete); it will remind the disciples of Jesus' words; like Jesus, it is sent by the Father.

The Spirit is known through inner experience, and this is the source of its importance. Shortly before the present passage, John's Jesus speaks of "the Spirit of truth, which the world cannot receive" and promises that it "remains with you and will be among you" (v. 17). Then Judas (not Iscariot), perceiving correctly the drift of this discussion, raises a difficult question: "What has happened [*or* Why has it happened] that you are going to manifest yourself to us and not to the world?" (The reader may recall the earlier statement in 3:17, to the effect that God sent the Son into the world to redeem the world.)

The lectionaries, unfortunately, omit Judas's question (v. 22), leaving Jesus' response in v. 23 without apparent motivation. The relationship of answer to question is a close one, however tangential it seems at first. When Jesus begins, "If any one loves me . . . ," he is saying, in effect, that he can be known only by those who love him. "If any one loves me, he will keep my word [*logos*, not the more ordinary term *rhema*]." "Keep" here means not only "obey," but "keep hold of," "preserve," "treasure up." And what is being kept here is not simply commandments, but *logos*, Jesus' own divine essence, of which the love commandment (compare the commentary above on the Gospel for the Fifth Sunday of Easter) is an aspect. Hence, Jesus' Father will love the one who keeps this *logos*, and the two of them will come and will take up residence with every

SIXTH SUNDAY OF EASTER 43

lover of the *logos*, for the *logos* belongs not to Jesus, but to the one who sent Jesus (v. 24).

It thus appears that the human failure to love can, in some sense, limit God's success with us. Only through love do we become open to the presence of God in and with us—a motif that will be stressed particularly in the lection for the Seventh Sunday of Easter. This love unites us so fully to the beloved that we can only rejoice in whatever good befalls the beloved, even if it means our separation: "If you loved me, you would be glad that I'm going to the Father" (v. 28). The love of the disciples is not yet perfect or complete, but John's Gospel does not reject them for that. The important thing is rather that love has begun to work its way in us.

The Spirit contributes to the growth of love in us by maintaining our connection with the beloved, even when the beloved is away. The Father will send the Spirit in Jesus' name, and the Spirit itself will not only teach the disciples all things, but bring to mind all the things that Jesus had told them. For the message of Jesus is not something to be learned and remembered merely as a form of words (indeed, Jesus seems not to have required his disciples to memorize his message). The impact of the message lay rather in its ability to change the hearer, to reveal new dimensions of reality, a new understanding of truth, and therefore a new way of living life. One can "remember" Jesus' message only as it proves its relevance by bringing about this process of conversion in the hearer.

Thus, conversion is itself a kind of remembering. We move to a new plane of understanding where familiar words gain new meaning and those that previously seemed irrelevant or unintelligible come to life again. The admission of uncircumcised Gentiles to the church, on which so many of the first lessons in Eastertide focus, marks such a conversion for the community as a whole. During this process, words of Jesus came to assume new meanings that had not been apparent in them before.

The context for the process of conversion is Jesus' gift of peace. It is not founded, like the world's peace, on ease of life, but rather on Jesus' having led the way through the sufferings inflicted by the world and returned, through them, to the Father. The peace Jesus leaves behind acknowledges the cross as well as the resurrection. It is characterized by change and growth and new life rather than unthinking and completely predictable stability. Yet, it is this peace that gives human beings real life in profound communion with God.

John 5:1-9. The Revised Common Lectionary also offers an alternative Gospel reading, the story of the paralytic whom Jesus heals at the Pool of Bethzatha. The story does have resonances with the Easter season. The man has been paralyzed for thirty-eight years and has been lying by the pool for quite some time without being able to avail himself of its healing powers. Jesus' raising of him is a sign of the creative power of the *logos*, who can act directly, bypassing the normal healing use of the waters. The motif of the pool may also suggest baptism, a major Eastertide theme. If so, it reminds us that while God provides sacraments for our use, God is not limited by them but can work directly with every soul for its salvation. This is a healthy corrective to certain triumphalist tendencies within the church, which has repeatedly tended to assert its own centrality to the process of salvation.

Ultimately, however, John's story of the paralytic is not a "success" story of conversion. In the episode that follows directly after the lection, the paralytic gratuitously betrays Jesus to the authorities (5:15-16). He functions more as an example of the unreliability of human response.

SECOND LESSON: REVELATION 21:10-14, 22—22:5

For a second lesson, the lectionaries have chosen various portions of Revelation 21 and 22: all materials having to do with the climactic vision of the New Jerusalem, the ideal human habitation, image of the age to come. This passage from Revelation presents the fulfillment of human existence in terms that evoke rich associations with the Scriptures of Israel, but that may sometimes seem arbitrary and peculiar to those who are not well-versed in them—including many modern Christian congregations.

The splendor of the heavenly city exceeds that of "Babylon," its earthly parody. The four-part symmetry of its gates serves to locate the city at the heart of the universe. The angels over the gates reverse the role of the cherubim who were posted, with the fiery sword, to keep humanity *out* of Eden after the Fall (Gen. 3:24). And each gate is inscribed with the name of one of the twelve tribes of Israel; for it is through Israel that humanity enters the heavenly city. At the same time, the foundations of the walls are inscribed with another series of twelve names—those of the twelve apostles of the Lamb. For the city comes into being not only through the relationship of God with Israel, but through the new and broader initiative of Jesus. One enters the city through the faith of Israel, but its foundations are the good news of God's enduring love for all humanity.

One great difference between the heavenly Jerusalem and its earthly counterpart is that the former contains no Temple (21:22). Since God is directly accessible to its inhabitants, a Temple would be superfluous, for a

SIXTH SUNDAY OF EASTER

Temple is needed only to localize a hidden and absent God in the difficult context of the present age.

God is not only the Temple of the New Jerusalem, but also its light, making sun and moon unnecessary as well (21:23). Here we have another reversal of Genesis. God created sun and moon to give light in this age (Gen. 1:14-19). Their disappearance serves to mark the contrast with the age to come. Note here and in the language about God as Temple that the Lamb (the risen Jesus) is associated intimately with God and, in effect, performs divine functions in the age to come. This surprisingly exalted language arises from the general perception of early Christians that Jesus played a critical role in humanity's interactions with God.

The seer goes on to emphasize the inclusion of the Gentiles (or "nations"; 21:24-26), who will walk in the city's light and bring their glory into it. Since there is no further hostility between Israelite and Gentile, the city has no further cause for fear. Its gates can stand open at all times, for there is no threat of war. The only things excluded from the city are "what is common [that is, unclean] and the person who commits abomination and lie" (21:27). These expressions can be read literally, of course, as reestablishing the Levitical purity code in the heavenly city. But John's emphasis on the presence of Gentiles militates against such a reading. It is more likely that here, as so often in the New Testament, the terms *common* and *abomination* (both of them purity terms) are being used metaphorically for unacceptable dispositions of the heart. Their equation here with the "lie" confirms this. [For a fuller exposition, see my book *Dirt, Greed and Sex: Sexual Ethics in the New Testament and Their Implications for Today* (Minneapolis: Fortress Press), 66–143.]

Finally, the Seer speaks of the throne of God and the Lamb and of the river that flows from it (22:1-5). Just as God is the Temple and the light of the city, God is also its source of life and health. For the river is flanked, on either side, by an orchard, and its trees are the tree of life! Remember that in the story of the Fall, God expelled the first parents from Eden precisely in order to keep them from this tree (Gen. 3:22).

The community of the New Jerusalem, then, is the community that humanity forfeited long ago through the Fall. But it is more than that. It is not simply the garden, as in Eden, but a garden in the midst of a city in the immediate and unending presence of God, who is the city's Temple. Those who live there, accordingly, are priests, as John has said earlier (1:6; 5:10; 20:6). The name of God, inscribed on their foreheads, reminds the reader of the golden plate bearing the words "Holy to the Lord" that the high priest of the earthly Temple wore on his forehead (Exod. 28:36-38).

FIRST LESSON: ACTS 14:8-18; 15:1-2, 22-29; 16:9-15; JOEL 2:21-27

The lectionaries diverge substantially in their choice of first reading, offering three quite different lections from Acts and one from Joel. The first of the Acts lections (*14:8-18*) is the story of Paul and Barnabas at Lystra, where they heal a man who could not walk and find themselves being greeted as manifestations of Zeus and Hermes. It is a captivating story in its own right, but is perhaps most interesting here in connection with the larger issue of inclusion of Gentiles in the Christian community. Inclusion did not mean that Gentiles were unchanged by their conversion or that Gentile culture was acceptable without further question. The problem was where to draw "the line."

The Pauline tradition drew it fairly loosely. Even in the matter of eating "foods sacrificed to idols," Paul stopped short of saying that it was categorically wrong, though he insisted that his addressees avoid giving scandal to others (1 Cor. 10:25-33). At the other extreme were those who demanded circumcision of male converts. The one thing that proved more or less inescapable, however, was that Gentiles could no longer worship their inherited gods, since there was no way to make sense of the unique importance of Jesus in that context. Even if conversion did not mean that Gentile Christians became Jewish in terms of their daily lives, it did mean that they became Jewish in terms of their understanding of God.

The second choice from Acts is a selection from the story of the Council of Jerusalem, telling of its initial occasion and giving a letter summarizing its decisions (*15:1-2, 22-29*). The topic, again, is Gentile converts. Against those who said that all Gentile males must be circumcised, the leaders meeting in Jerusalem decide that the Gentiles need keep only a rather "light" list of purity rules: abstention from foods sacrificed to idols, from blood, perhaps from the meat of strangled animals (the text is uncertain), and from "fornication" (15:29). The meaning of the food rules is fairly clear; the precise meaning of "fornication," however, is impossible to determine with complete confidence, since the word can mean a variety of things. One possibility is that it refers literally to some forbidden range of sexual acts, perhaps to marriages considered incestuous by Jews. Another possibility is that it is used metaphorically to mean participation in non-Jewish religious rites—a usage fairly common in the Scriptures of Israel. In any case, the decision of the Council, according to Luke, was more restrictive than the requirements laid down in Paul's letters.

The third choice (*Acts 16:9-15*) tells about Paul's nighttime vision of a man saying, "Come over to Macedonia and help us!" Luke explains that this was interpreted as a divine vocation and that it led to the first preaching of the gospel in Europe. The main part of the lection, however, is devoted to the important figure of Lydia the purple-merchant, the first convert in Europe. She was apparently a Gentile God-fearer (that is, one who had adopted the Jewish understanding of God) in a community without any substantial Jewish population. It is her enthusiasm and insistent hospitality that grounds the first European church community mentioned in the New Testament.

The lection from *Joel 2:21-27* is a celebration of the return of prosperity after drought and locusts (1:1—2:11). The early and latter rains bring the hope of new crops, and Joel summons the people, who have been in mourning before the Lord (2:12-17), to rejoice in the evidence of God's kindness. The promise of renewed life is consonant with the most basic themes of Eastertide and the imagery is concrete and powerful. Since it is designed to be used with Acts 14:8-18, it reaffirms the theme of the One God as life-giver in contradistinction to any other powers that might claim divine authority.

The Ascension of Our Lord

Lectionary	First Lesson	Psalm	Second Lesson	Gospel
Revised Common	Acts 1:1-11	Psalm 47 or Psalm 110	Eph. 1:15-23	Luke 24:44-53
Episcopal (BCP)	Acts 1:1-11 or 2 Kings 2:1-15	Psalm 47 or Ps. 110:1-5	Eph. 1:15-23 or Acts 1:1-11	Luke 24:49-53 or Mark 16:9-15, 19-20
Roman Catholic	Acts 1:1-11	Ps. 47:2-3, 6-9	Heb. 9:24-28; 10:19-23	Luke 24:46-53
Lutheran (LBW)	Acts 1:1-11	Psalm 110	Eph. 1:16-23	Luke 24:44-53

GOSPEL: LUKE 24:44-53

The basic organizing principle for the Ascension Day lections is the pairing of the end of Luke's Gospel with the beginning of Acts. Accordingly, I will discuss these two lections first, before taking up the alternatives to them and the second lessons. There is an artful overlap between the two, serving to connect the two volumes of Luke's work. The story of the ascension is first sketched briefly at the end of the Gospel, then told in more detail at the beginning of Acts. Other resources are of less utility for the occasion, since Luke is the only author who specifies the fortieth day after the resurrection as the occasion of a specific event he calls the ascension. Other references to Jesus' ascension are more vague. In John's Gospel, it is barely mentioned as part of Jesus' return to the Father (20:17). The account in the "long ending" of Mark's Gospel is probably a summary of Luke's. Elsewhere, the ascension is little more than an implication of the Heavenly Session of Christ—his being seated at the right hand of God.

The difficulty that many preachers find in proclaiming the ascension is probably related to all this. It is nowhere treated as a saving moment, on the order of the cross or the resurrection. That Luke makes a major issue of it, one suspects, owes something to the requirements of his plot. He needs a clean break between the story of Jesus and the story of the church, with Jesus clearly off the scene as a protagonist (though reappearing in visions). No other evangelist faced such a need. At an earlier time, one gathers from Paul that there was no sharp distinction between the appearances of Jesus directly following the resurrection and later appearances like his own experience on the way to Damascus (1 Cor. 15:1-11).

The story of the ascension, then, as we have it is probably a creation of Luke's. For his willingness to create such scenes, compare his version of Jesus' visit to Nazareth (4:14-30) with its probable source in Mark 6:1-6. There, he has lengthened the Markan narrative, changed its focus, and moved it from the middle to the beginning of Jesus' ministry. We do not know Luke's sources for the story of the ascension, but we can at least see that he shaped the story to serve as a bridge element between his two volumes. It removes Jesus effectively from the immediate scene and prepares the way for the era of the church.

This function called for clear contours, easily grasped by the reader or hearer of Luke's narrative. It is the very sharpness of these contours that renders the narrative hard to translate into the terms of later eras. Luke worked in terms of a cosmology that understood the earth as a sphere at the center of the cosmos, with the heavens surrounding it as concentric spheres, carrying the moon, sun, planets, and fixed stars. There was no conception of "outer space" as a frigid and lifeless void. Instead, the regions stretching upward toward the ultimate sky or heaven (that of the fixed stars) was conceived as fully inhabitable for human beings. The idea of Jesus ascending through these spheres to a heavenly throne presented no great difficulties to Luke or his hearers. (For a more detailed picture of Hellenistic cosmology—still quite alive in the Middle Ages—see C. S. Lewis's *The Discarded Image: An Introduction to Medieval and Renaissance Literature* [New York: Cambridge University Press, 1994].)

The preacher who hopes to find some proclamation of the gospel in the story may have to move away from Luke's own literalization of it and back toward the vaguer notion of ascension as return to intimacy with God, as one finds it in John. One can do so with justice to Luke by noting the theological points that he has built into his telling of the story: fulfillment of Scripture, the disciples as witnesses, the sending of the Spirit, the sorrow of parting from Jesus, the joy of the disciples, and their eager participation in the worship of God.

The point, for Luke, is not the discontinuity of Jesus' arrival or departure, but the continuity that bridges both. Luke sees Jesus' life as breathing the same air as ancient Israel. The opening chapters of his Gospel are redolent of it: the aged couple with no child, the angelic appearances that announce important births, the centrality of the Temple, the presence of prophets, male and female. For Luke, much of the meaning of Jesus consists in this intimate connection to the past, which Jesus now brings to completion. But equally, much of it consists in the way Jesus' ministry leads on to that of the church. The church continues Jesus' ministry by testifying to what it has seen and remembered of Jesus' own life and by experiencing the indwelling of the Spirit, which enables the believers to speak powerfully and to work miracles like Jesus. Even when deprived of Jesus' immediate presence, the church responds with joy and praise because it knows that human life has been changed by Jesus' work.

FIRST LESSON: ACTS 1:1-11

The related account at the beginning of Acts starts with a short dedication to one Theophilus, also the dedicatee of the Gospel (Luke 1:1-4). The brief repetition of such dedications may have helped the reader identify volumes belonging to a single work. In this case, the dedication also underlines the way the ascension functions in the structure of the two books: the first discourse covered Jesus' acts and teaching until the day when he was "taken up" (v. 2). Acts will begin from this pivotal moment.

How, then, does the ascension determine the character of what is to follow—the history of the spread of the gospel and the church? Perhaps there is at least a hint in the references to the Second Coming, which appears to be the other, often unnoticed, preoccupation of the passage. The subject is raised twice: first by the disciples in conversation with Jesus (vv. 6-8), then by the angels at the end of the story (vv. 10-11).

In the first instance, the disciples ask Jesus, "Is this the time when you restore the kingdom to Israel?" Jesus responds by telling them that it is not for them to know the times and seasons. The Father has·determined these in his own authority. While Luke's Jesus does not deny knowledge of them himself (as he does, for example, in Mark 13:32), he leaves them in the Father's hands. If the disciples, then, are not to know the times or seasons, what is their role? "But," says Jesus—using the strong adversative *alla*, not the ambiguous *de*—"you will receive power when the Holy Spirit has come upon you, and you will be my witnesses in Jerusalem and in all Judea and Samaria and to the end of the earth." In short, there is a strong contrast set up between the eschatological expectation that interests itself in times and seasons and the kind of Spirit-empowered witness that is to characterize the work of the church. Luke's Jesus puts the latter in place of the former.

Given that, it seems odd, at first, that the angels return to the subject of the Second Coming in their speech to the disciples after Jesus' departure: "Why do you stand looking into heaven? This Jesus who's been taken up from you into heaven will come in just the same way as you saw him going into heaven" (v. 11). At first glance, this might appear to be a reason to *continue* gazing into the heavens. The key issue, though, is that the ascension was beyond the disciples' control. Similarly, the return will be beyond their control. Though it will certainly come, there is no point in gawking after it. The only thing a faithful disciple can do is wait, as commanded, for the gift of the Spirit and practice the role of witness as only disciples can do. After the ascension, Jesus continues to be the subject matter of the narrative, since the disciples' task is to witness to him and to his significance for the world.

ALTERNATIVE GOSPEL: MARK 16:9-15, 19-20

As already pointed out, the combination of Luke and Acts provides the basic "skeleton" of the Ascension Day readings. The *BCP* lectionary, however, provides an alternative for the Gospel reading: Mark 16:9-15, 19-20. These verses come from the "long ending" of Mark's Gospel, which is not found in a number of manuscripts, including the two generally esteemed most highly: Sinaiticus and Vaticanus. The style, moreover, seems quite un-Markan, not only in its vocabulary, but in its tendency to give summary reports of events, which contrasts with Mark's habit of giving narratives in an expansive form. Given the modern recognition that the original form of Mark (or, at least, the oldest form we have) probably ended at 16:8, with the women's frightened departure from the tomb, Mark 16:9-20 may perhaps now be considered of secondary canonicity. Modern translations tend to set it apart from the rest of Mark's Gospel. I know of no official church pronouncements regarding its authority, but I suspect that it has declined, de facto, for many Christians to a status not unlike that of the Old Testament Apocrypha in Anglicanism: suitable to read in church, but not to be relied on for major matters of faith.

This passage does, however, contain the only other New Testament reference to the ascension as a distinct and concrete event, in the sense Luke has given it. It is interesting, then, to note the context in which the lection places this event. It comes as the conclusion and climax of the resurrection appearances. And the point that "Mark" stresses throughout is that the Eleven have displayed a notable lack of faith. They did not believe Mary Magdalene, nor the "people going into the country" (perhaps Luke's two travelers to Emmaus). And when Jesus at last appears to the Eleven, he reproves them for their slowness to believe. Even if this passage is not by Mark, the author has retained Mark's suspicion of the Twelve and his insistence that it is the minor characters, outsiders to one degree or another, who see Jesus more truly.

The lection is edited to omit the verses detailing the "signs following," which were to authenticate the witness of the Eleven once they finally get moving. The fear that these verses might give comfort to snake-handling cults may be the reason why the long ending of Mark has been allowed to slip into oblivion in many denominations. And yet, a careful reading of the passage suggests that Mark is not speaking about repeatable Christian rituals, but about occasional miraculous works bestowed by God as co-worker and strengthener of the message. The transposition of such gifts into ritual may even be an effort to take them out of God's hands and appropriate them to the worshiper's own control and use—rather the opposite of what "Mark" suggests.

SECOND LESSON: EPHESIANS 1:15-23; HEBREWS 9:24-28; 10:19-23

Most of the lectionaries draw their second reading from *Ephesians 1:15-23*, especially its reference to the Heavenly Session in vv. 20-23. This image comes originally from Psalm 110:1, where the placement of the king at God's right hand identifies the king as God's second-in-command. Similarly, Jesus, in this passage, is God's plenipotentiary for all dealings with the created world, even with the various ranks of angelic powers listed in v. 21. The author of the letter insists that there is nothing that is outside the authority of the risen Christ, now or in the age to come.

Moreover, the church will participate in Jesus' authority. God "has made him head over all things *for the church*, which is his body, the fullness of the one who is filling all in all" (vv. 22b-23). This is not a promise of institutional power for the church, but a claim that the order of salvation creates the existing world anew, abolishing its hostilities and replacing them with a single new humanity (cf. 2:14). It is this new humanity that receives the promise.

The theme of the Heavenly Session here is thus focused rather differently from Luke's theme of Ascension. The point is not to remove Jesus from the present scene so much as to assert that the gospel message has ultimate power behind it and must ultimately triumph, not as a new faction within humanity but as a renewal of all humanity.

The lesson from *Hebrews 9:24-28; 10:19-23* also refers to Jesus' entry into heaven, but in a priestly rather than a royal capacity. He enters, as high priest, into the true Holy of Holies with his own blood as offering, in order to reestablish communion with God by taking away the sins that have impeded it. The presence of Jesus in this role gives us confidence to enter the sanctuary along with him. The focus is future, but it is not without implications for life here and now, for to be Christian means to have been initiated into a new kind of existence—"sprinkled" from bad conscience and "washed" in clean water.

ALTERNATIVE FIRST LESSON: 2 KINGS 2:1-15

Finally, the *BCP* lectionary offers, as an alternative first lesson, the story of the ascension of Elijah in 2 Kings 2. The choice might seem almost too obvious, since it comprises the principal literary source for the motif of ascension in Luke-Acts. The interest of pairing this reading with Acts and Luke lies in its tracing of Elisha's response to the event. He cleaves to his teacher and does not want to let him go. He tears his clothes after Elijah's

THE ASCENSION OF OUR LORD 53

departure (v. 12) as if mourning the dead, for the pain of separation is the same. Yet, because of his attentiveness even through the moment of bereavement, he is granted a gift of Spirit. The tension between loss and gain, bereavement and empowerment, evoked in Luke is perhaps even more clearly stated here.

Seventh Sunday of Easter

Lectionary	First Lesson	Psalm	Second Lesson	Gospel
Revised Common	Acts 16:16-34	Psalm 97	Rev. 22:12-14, 16-17, 20-21	John 17:20-26
Episcopal (BCP)	Acts 16:16-34 or 1 Sam. 12:19-24	Ps. 68:1-20 or Psalm 47	Rev. 22:12-14, 16-17, 20 or Acts 16:16-34	John 17:20-26
Roman Catholic	Acts 7:55-60	Ps. 97:1-2, 6-7, 9	Rev. 22:12-14, 16-17, 20	John 17:20-26
Lutheran (LBW)	Acts 16:6-10	Psalm 47	Rev. 22:12-17, 20	John 17:20-26

GOSPEL: JOHN 17:20-26

In the first half of John's Gospel, there is a pattern made up of events followed by discourses on related themes. The feeding of the multitude (6:5-15), for example, is followed by the discourse on the true bread (6:26-59). From the middle of the Gospel onward, however, the sequence reverses itself. The brief discourse on light (9:1-5) immediately precedes the healing of the man born blind; and the Good Shepherd discourse, with its motifs of calling the sheep by name and giving them eternal life (10:3, 27), precedes the raising of Lazarus. John suggests at the very beginning of the last supper discourses that they are related to the passion and resurrection narratives that will follow, which he calls Jesus' "crossing over" into God (13:1). When we read the great prayer of John 17, then, we should bear in mind that it relates to these events.

The prayer belongs to the context of Jesus' departure, the same issue being grappled with in the readings for Ascension Day. It envisions an ongoing community that will live in future generations of believers. As in the Ephesians reading for Ascension Day, this is a community in intimate relationship to Jesus. But where the author of Ephesians refers to the church as Jesus' body, John uses the more mystical language of Jesus being "in" the believers and the believers being "in" Jesus and "in" God.

The prayer of John 17 is sometimes read as the charter of the modern ecumenical movement. This is not entirely wrong. John does expect that the believers' unity with Jesus and God and with one another will have perceptible consequences, for he writes of this unity as a sign to the "world." In Johannine terms, the world is the creation in its refusal to acknowledge its created nature, trying to be self-sufficient and fully in control. This world can be *saved*—that is, brought back to a true and honest relationship with its Maker. If that in us which is "world" can perceive the consequences of the believers' union with God through Christ, perhaps it will understand and accept its own createdness and so return.

Still, the modern image of "church unity" is a misleading one. For one thing, it is too institutional a model. "Church union" tends to mean merger of ministerial orders and bureaucracies. The Johannine literature in the New Testament is distinguished for its lack of interest in such matters. It is *very* interested in the unity of the believing community, but it expresses this interest rather in a concern for how Christians actively treat one another. In 1 John, the secessionist group is accused, at least indirectly, of not loving the brother or sister whom they have seen—in which case they cannot love the God whom they have not seen (1 John 4:16b-21). In both John and 1 John, the love commandment is phrased as "love one another," thus emphasizing love as the supremely characteristic mark of the believing community.

Interpretation of John 17 in terms of "church unity" is also too shallow. It speaks only of the consequences of the love evoked here, not of its source. The source is our profound intimacy with Jesus and with God. Being united with God in Jesus, the believer is also united with all other believers. The inner life of the believing community is actually an experience of the life of God. Jesus prays "that they may be one just as you, Father, are in me and I in you." This echoes the language John's Jesus used earlier, in the Good Shepherd discourse: "I and the Father are one" (10:30). It is related to the riddling language of the Prologue: "And the *logos* was with God, and the *logos* was God" (1:1). The *logos* can be thought as both identical with God and distinct from God. This divine difference-in-unity, a mystical union without loss of distinct identity, is the model for the believer's intimacy with God and with the believing community.

The unity for which John's Jesus prays, then, is not a *duty* but a direct expression of the spiritual experience of the believers. The modern interpreter of John should not settle for "church unity" as the goal. Even if it may be a valid and worthy interim objective, it is too low an aim to reflect the true meaning of this prayer. The true aim is transformation of the believers through our intimate and loving experience of God so that we can begin to see others as intimately related to us and to behave in an actively loving way within the community.

Even here, the point is not for Christian love to stop with the community but for it to become a sign to the "world" of what is possible in a human life immersed in intimacy with God. This is the purpose of the incarnation: "God so loved the world as to give his only Son so that everyone who believes in him might not perish but have eternal life" (3:16). "Eternal life" is not merely something in the age to come (which John does not much emphasize); it is the power of divine life already here and now. Similarly, the passion and resurrection are means to the same end. Jesus says, "And I, if I am lifted up from the earth, will draw all people to myself" (12:32). This is not primarily about "church" in the everyday institutional sense; it is about enjoying the life of the age to come—eternal life, in John's language—here and now.

SECOND LESSON: REVELATION 22:12-17, 20-21

The second lesson is drawn from the end of Revelation—the closing dialogue between Jesus and the Seer. The risen Jesus speaks of himself here in terms that belong more to the divine than to the human: "I am the alpha and the omega [a phrase used by God in 1:8], the first and the last, the beginning and the end" (22:13). The ensuing interchange is complex, as it pulls together many of the themes used earlier in the work, but the primary emphasis is on the prospect of an imminent second coming: "Behold, I am coming quickly" (v. 12); "Yes, I am coming quickly" (v. 20). The seer, on behalf of the persecuted community, greets this prospect with joy: "The Spirit and the bride say, 'Come'; and let the one who hears say, 'Come'" (v. 17); "Amen, come, Lord Jesus!" (v. 20). The prospect of Jesus' coming is also a prospect of judgment. Some will be given the right to the tree of life (v. 14); others will be shut out (v. 15). In the meantime, there is the witness of the Seer (v. 16) to offer encouragement to endangered churches, water to the thirsty (v. 17), and "the grace of the Lord Jesus" to sustain the weary (v. 21).

As with all the readings from Revelation this Eastertide, the preacher is challenged by the vividness of the language, which often transcends the cultural distance between its own time and today, in contrast with the particularity of the original social context of the work and the fact that its apparent expectation of a literal, imminent end of the world was disappointed. Nowhere is this tension more obvious than in the present passage. It is not respectful of the sacred text to suggest that the Spirit, speaking through the Seer, was indifferent to the misleading character of such language. It may satisfy those who have the benefit of hindsight to refer to 2 Peter 3:8: "One day, with the Lord, is like a thousand years, and a thousand years as one day." But it is impossible to think that the first readers would not have taken these words literally. Revelation was either factually wrong in its prediction or morally wrong in the way it expressed itself.

Yet, the power of the words remains because they respond to a perennial sense of urgency in human life, not least evident in our own era, when

SEVENTH SUNDAY OF EASTER

the rapidity of social and technological change has given us a sense of being caught in a flood, with familiar landmarks being swallowed up all around us. The gospel answer to this sense of anxiety is, in fact, the resurrection of Jesus, with its promise that our experience, even at its most painful and disastrous, is not without purpose or direction. If Jesus is the beginning, he is also the end (or goal, *telos*) (v. 13). He is altogether human, "the root and clan of David" (v. 16)—and therefore one of us. And for exactly this reason, he is also "the bright morning star" (v. 16) that guides us into the life of the age to come.

There has been and is an age-long argument between Christians who want to use Revelation to calculate the "times and seasons" (something Luke's Jesus specifically places off-limits to his followers in Acts 1:7!) and those who have been suspicious at best of Revelation and its interpreters (the work had a hard time getting and maintaining a place in the canon of the New Testament). But the power of the imagery finally defeats both groups. It conveys, after all, a great message of hope that transcends the work's own mistakes in dating the end of the world. For the message is focused not on the accuracy of any specific dating, but on confidence in the God who raised Jesus and belief that "the Lamb that was slain" is also the key to the most bounteous and courageous human existence, both in this world and in the age to come.

FIRST LESSON: ACTS 16:6-10, 16-34; 7:55-60; I SAMUEL 12:19-24

The lectionaries exhibit little agreement about the first lesson for today. Two of them agree in choosing part of the Philippi narrative in Acts 16. The politics of the story are interesting—the way a financial grievance leads to public charges of introducing wrongful customs and the way Paul and Silas's astonishing refusal to flee brings about the conversion of their jailer. But the element that is particularly interesting in *Acts 16:16-34*, given that this is the Sunday before Pentecost, may be the conflict between Paul's mission and the prophetic spirit that has possessed the slave-woman.

The early Christians seem not to have had such sharply defined beliefs about the Holy Spirit as their successors. Both Paul (1 Cor. 14:32) and the Johannine community (1 John 4:1-3) assumed that there were multiple spirits behind the phenomenon of prophecy in the church. Luke emphasizes the role of the Holy Spirit more than most, but is willing to acknowledge that even a spirit operating within a purely pagan context (Luke calls it a *python*, alluding to the Delphic oracle) might in fact recognize and speak the truth.

Paul's exasperation in the story has less to do with the spirit's identifying them than with the fact that it follows them for "many days." This spirit speaks the truth, but hampers the mission. The quality of resurrection, however, pervades Paul's work. It is impossible for it to go entirely wrong, even when his exorcism of the slave-woman provokes a legal assault on him by her owners, a beating, and a night in jail. The whole experience leads to the proclamation of the gospel to the jailer and his family.

For the reading from *Acts 16:6-10*, see the treatment of part of this text above, under the Sixth Sunday of Easter; but note also the reference to the Holy Spirit's role in steering Paul's party toward Europe by *preventing* them from preaching the word in the province of Asia. The Spirit may work by restraining as well as encouraging, by prohibition as well as exhortation.

Acts 7:55-60 gives us Stephen's vision of the ascended Jesus standing at the right hand of God's glory. The lection combines this visionary confirmation of the ascension with the assurance that Stephen was "full of the Holy Spirit," thus providing an allusion to the feast of Pentecost as well. Stephen, in the story, has already angered the court with his radicalism about the Temple, and his description of his vision pushes them over the brink into becoming a lynch mob. (Luke depicts all court proceedings that condemn Christians as involving serious lapses of justice.) Stephen dies in a way that mirrors the death of Jesus in at least some versions of Luke 23:34—forgiving those who have harmed him. And his death serves the narrator's need to introduce Saul—who will be profoundly affected, in his turn, by a meeting with the risen Lord (9:1-9).

The reasons for the choice of *1 Samuel 12:19-24* are not obvious. Presumably they have to do with the motif of Samuel continuing to pray for the people (v. 23), which is echoed in the Gospel lection for today. The context, however, is quite different, for this is part of the larger narrative that accounts for the shift from rule by judges to a monarchy in Israel— which it treats as an act of apostasy. Still, there is a kind of departure, for Samuel is alienated from the people and will withdraw from active leadership. And the passage reasserts God's relationship to the chosen people, despite their sin, and the need for faithfulness on the people's part. All these are elements consistent with the larger context of Jesus' prayer in John's Gospel.

Pentecost Sunday
The Day of Pentecost/Whitsunday

Lectionary	First Lesson	Psalm	Second Lesson	Gospel
Revised Common	Acts 2:1-21 or Gen. 11:1-9	Ps. 104:24-34, 35b	Rom. 8:14-17 or Acts 2:1-21	John 14:8-17, (25-27)
Episcopal (BCP)	Acts 2:1-11 or Joel 2:28-32	Ps. 104:25-37 or 104:25-32 or 33:12-15, 18-22	1 Cor. 12:4-13 or Acts 2:1-11	John 20:19-23 or John 14:8-17
Roman Catholic	Acts 2:1-11	Ps. 104:1, 24, 29-31, 34	Rom. 8:8-17	John 14:15-16, 23b-26
Lutheran (LBW)	Gen. 11:1-9	Ps. 104:25-34	Acts 2:1-21	John 15:26-27; 16:4b-11

FIRST LESSON: ACTS 2:1-21

The reading from Acts 2 is the central reading for Pentecost, since it narrates the event being celebrated. Accordingly, we will discuss it first. Like the forty days of resurrection appearances and like the ascension story, the giving of the Spirit on Pentecost is found nowhere in the New Testament outside the works of Luke. Any understanding of its meaning, then, must take account of how Luke is construing it as part of his larger narrative. We have already seen that the commandment to wait in Jerusalem for the gift of "power from on high" is part of Luke's ascension narrative (Luke 24:49; Acts 1:8). The choice of the fortieth day after the resurrection for Jesus' ascension and the fiftieth for the giving of the Spirit was no doubt determined partly by the associations of the two numbers.

Forty is the traditional number for preparatory or transitional periods. Compare the forty days and nights of rain and the forty days of flood in the story of Noah. Both Isaac and Esau were forty when they married. Moses was on the mountain for forty days and nights. The wilderness wandering lasted forty years. The spies returned from Canaan after forty days. The list is a long one and includes Jesus' own forty days in the wilderness in Luke 4:2. When applied to the resurrection appearances, the number implies not completion, but transition and expectation. The resurrection is not its own reason for being; it is preparation for something more—a something more that can appropriately be indicated by the number fifty.

What is called "fifty days" on inclusive reckoning is forty-nine days if one omits the starting point from the count. The Israelite pilgrimage feast that in Greek was called "Pentecost" (Fifty) in Hebrew was "Shavuoth" (Weeks). The Feast of Weeks took place a week of weeks (49 days) after Passover. In itself, seven is a number of completeness. It includes not only

59

the creation of the world but God's rest at the end of that work. It is the number of days in Passover and the number it takes to ordain a priest. Matthew reckons the genealogy of Jesus as including six times seven generations from Abraham (Matt. 1:17), leaving Jesus to introduce the seventh seven. The giving of the Spirit, then, on the fiftieth day after the resurrection represents for Luke the completion of something to which the forty days of Jesus' postresurrection presence was preparatory.

We have already seen that, for Luke, the disciples are to be witnesses, communicating the good news of Jesus' acts and teachings. The gift of the Spirit, then, is appropriately a gift of speech. Wind becomes breath; tongues of fire become tongues of language. This sounds at first like the kind of "speaking in tongues" that Paul writes about in 1 Corinthians 12–14. It may well allude to that practice, but it is not quite the same. Where Paul complains that "speaking in tongues" will be unintelligible to outsiders (1 Cor. 14:23-25), Luke describes the speech of the disciples on Pentecost as intelligible even to those who would not have expected it to be (Acts 2:11).

There is some difficulty in interpreting who the audience is in vv. 5-11. They are described as "Jews, pious men from every nation under heaven." Despite the presence of the term *nation,* with its hint of Gentile identity, this description actually suggests an entirely Jewish audience (albeit one including proselytes); and indeed it is too early in Luke's narrative for Gentile converts (that begins only with Peter's conversion of the household of Cornelius in Acts 10). Even acknowledging that the audience has far-flung sources, ranging from Parthia and Elam in the east to Rome in the west, from Arabia in the south to Pontus in the north, it appears that the Jewish inhabitants of these places would all have spoken either Greek or Aramaic or both. Since both languages were current in Galilee, the event does not seem quite so startling, after all. Or was it simply the use of both languages by one group that seemed startling? After all, in the remainder of Acts, Luke will suggest a fairly sharp division between Greek-speaking and Aramaic-speaking Jews, even within the Christian community.

In any case, Luke is presenting us with a miracle of *communication.* The primary point is not to impress with the apparent impossibility of the event but to communicate a message about the "great things of God" (v. 11). To speak and to be understood—this is the great gift of the Spirit. Yet, the result of the gift, in this imperfect world, turns out to be division—also a characteristic theme of Luke's (compare Simeon's prophecy, Luke 2:34-35). Some take the event seriously, though they are perplexed by it. Others dismiss it as evidence of drunkenness. Out of this conflict emerges Peter's Pentecost sermon.

The lection, even in its longer form, can accommodate only part of Peter's speech, primarily the quotation from Joel 2. Luke has interpreted the quotation by adding a reference to "the last days," that is, the time of fulfillment that is now beginning. But it is otherwise taken over in a fairly straightforward form. It makes a striking example of the way the early Christians, returning to the Scriptures with new perspectives, found in them a witness to their own experience. The prophecy is striking, too, for its social breadth—including even slaves among those who will receive the outpouring of Spirit—and for the way it combines the threat of judgment with the hope of salvation for those who call upon the name of the Lord.

Thus the outpouring of the Spirit is for the sake of salvation, not condemnation, as Peter will make clear further on in the story (vv. 37-39). Luke sees it as the foundation of all the witnessing and evangelizing that will fill the remaining pages of Acts. It allows the believers to speak with "boldness" (*parrhesia*), a characteristic of those who have nothing to fear and nothing to hide (v. 29). This event is not, for Luke, the "birthday of the church," for the community of the disciples already existed and was taking responsibility for its life (Acts 1:12-26); but it is the moment when the church comes into its own as witness and evangelist. In that sense, it is a moment not merely of preparation but of fulfillment—the fiftieth and not the fortieth day.

GOSPEL: JOHN 14:8-17, 23b-27; 15:26-27; 16:4b-11; 20:19-23

The most broadly favored choice of Gospel lection (*John 14:8-17*) continues two themes already explored in the readings for previous Sundays: the unity of Jesus and the Father (vv. 9-11); and the "Spirit of Truth" as "another Paraclete," whom the disciples will recognize but the world cannot receive (vv. 16-17). It is particularly significant that the Spirit is here designated as "Spirit of Truth," for rejection of truth is precisely what makes us "world" in the negative sense of the term. Only cultivation of truthfulness enables one to recognize truth. Even the disciples can recognize truth only insofar as it inhabits them and remains among them. (This teaching brings the Jesus of John's Gospel very close to the Jesus of the Synoptics with his attacks on hypocrisy.)

The connection between the reassertion of Jesus' oneness with the Father in vv. 8-11 and the giving of the Spirit in vv. 15-17 is hardly accidental. What connects them is the keeping of "my commandments," meaning above all the command to love one another. As in the prayer of John 17, communion with God depends on love, which alone disposes the believer to the kind of intimacy that constitutes union with God and with other believers.

The connecting verses, however, also make the astonishing promise that those who believe in Jesus will do greater things than he has done. Even though all prayer flows to the Father through the name of Jesus and all power flows from the Father through the gift of Jesus, it does not follow that the disciples are only pale copies of Jesus and the Father. As John's Jesus says to them elsewhere, "You are my friends" (15:14). Friends are taken as equals, even if they do not originate as such. We are pleased that our friends retain their individuality and their accomplishments. A true friend does not begrudge these. So, too, with John's Jesus: His departure, through the cross and resurrection, is not only an end but a beginning. It affirms the distinctive potential of Jesus' friends.

(For the extensions of this Gospel lection into the latter part of chapter 14, see the discussion of the lection for the Sixth Sunday of Easter.)

For the lection from *John 20:19-23*, see the commentary on the same text for the Second Sunday of Easter. Since this was the prescribed reading on that Sunday, the preacher following the *BCP* lectionary might do well to take the option of John 14:8-17 for today. The preacher who chooses John 20:19-23 should note that it treats the giving of the Spirit quite differently from Acts, placing it on Easter Sunday and giving it the form of Jesus' breath rather than the tongues of fire and wind. Reading the two narratives together, however, will give the preacher an opportunity to talk about how these two writers have clothed the intimate connection between Jesus, the Spirit, and the Christian people in such different forms.

The *LBW* chooses *John 15:26-27; 16:4b-11*. This lection emphasizes the connection between Jesus' departure and the giving of the Spirit. It also speaks of the Spirit in relation to the fact that human beings cannot know everything at once. Even Jesus' discourse has to take account of the particular moment (16:4b); some things can now be said that were not appropriate before. Jesus' imminent departure will change the situation still further, since it will be the ultimate demonstration of the world's sin (that is, its refusal to acknowledge its created status), of Jesus' and of God's righteousness (for what the world thinks of as its triumph in crucifying him is really his return to glory), and of judgment (for the ruler of this world, that is, the devil, the liar, has failed). Hence the Spirit will play out its role under circumstances different from those of Jesus' ministry, making new kinds of insight possible.

ALTERNATIVE FIRST LESSON: GENESIS 11:1-9; JOEL 2:28-32

The lectionaries provide a broad variety of other readings to accompany Acts and John. The story of Babel (*Genesis 11:1-9*) is an appropriate choice to go with the lesson from Acts, since Luke presents Pentecost as reversing the effects of Babel. The Spirit brings the gift of intelligibility where the sin of arrogance at Babel brought down a judgment of unintelligibility. The people once "scattered . . . abroad over the face of all the earth" are now reunited in Jerusalem, hearing the praises of God spoken in their own tongues.

The reading from *Joel 2:28-32* is the passage quoted in the longer form of the lection from Acts 2. It is meant to accompany the shorter form of that lection in the *BCP* lectionary (see the comments on this material in the discussion of Acts 2 above). The preacher who wants to have this material available and also take advantage of the epistle reading from 1 Corinthians can simply extend the Acts reading through verse 21.

SECOND LESSON: ROMANS 8:8-17; 2 CORINTHIANS 12:4-13

The reading from *Romans 8:8-17* offers a more "personal" interpretation of the meaning of the Spirit. Where Luke is interested in a kind of world-historical role for the Spirit as introducing an age of fulfillment, Romans relates the giving of the Spirit more to the believer's experience of the life of faith. The shorter form of the reading, used in the Revised Common Lectionary, focuses on the sense of adoption, of sharing Jesus' immediate relationship with God as Abba. This is a spirituality of intimacy not unlike that of John.

The longer version of the Romans reading includes a contrast between flesh and spirit as conflicting elements within the human being. This language is very open to misunderstanding. Some Christians have interpreted it to mean that the source of evil in the human being resides literally in the flesh. Taken to its logical limit, such an approach leads to a Gnostic rejection of the material world. It is more likely that Paul is using "flesh" and "spirit" metaphorically of opposing tendencies within the human being. When "the Spirit of the one who raised Jesus from the dead" dwells in us, it can give true life to the mortal body. Here, too, the language of indwelling brings the thought close to that of John.

Finally, the reading from *1 Corinthians 12:4-13* explores yet another arena of the Spirit's working—its provision for the life of the church. Paul calls on the Spirit to provide a principle of unity-in-diversity. The varying gifts of the members of the community are not to be ascribed to diverse spirits. Quite the contrary, one Spirit supplies what is needed for the whole church by giving varying gifts to the individual members. This means that the gifts of the Spirit are not for the prestige or gratification of the person who receives them. Rather, the recipient of the gift holds it "for the benefit [of the whole]." This may be the most important aspect of the doctrine of the Spirit for development in the late twentieth century as churches struggle to make room for diversity in their membership despite inherited presuppositions that all members of the church should ascribe to a rather uniform culture or code of conduct, usually of European derivation. The Spirit creates a rich and articulate life for the ongoing church in its life of witness and endows it with all the gifts it needs.